An American Philosophy of Social Security

# AN AMERICAN PHILOSOPHY OF SOCIAL SECURITY

## *Evolution and Issues*

J. DOUGLAS BROWN

PRINCETON UNIVERSITY PRESS
PRINCETON, NEW JERSEY

This book has been set in Linotype Times Roman

Printed in the United States of America
by Princeton University Press

# Foreword

IT HAS BEEN the author's intention in writing *An American Philosophy of Social Security* to assist the concerned layman in understanding one of the most important developments in American social legislation in this century. The book is neither a technical analysis nor a detailed history, but attempts the more difficult task of distilling from the author's involvement in the planning of the social security program since its beginnings an organized series of concise essays which emphasize the broad sweep of evolution of the system and the major issues which have been resolved or are still to be decided.

To maintain the momentum of discussion, the author has frequently exercised severe restraint in condensing into a paragraph or two technical detail or legislative history which could fill pages. At other times, to give a sense of reality, especially in respect to early critical events, these have been described more fully. Since the primary purpose of the monograph is to help in the general understanding of the philosophy and policy of social security, and not to serve the specialist in social insurance administration, many specific applications of policy have been passed over. The test of inclusion or omission has been relevance to the author's purpose to give the reader a balanced exposition of the reasons why the system is in its present form and why further evolution is necessary.

While occasional reference is made to unemployment insurance and workmen's compensation insurance, the book is built around the integrated national system of social security which includes Old Age, Survivors, and

Disability Insurance (OASDI) and Hospital and Medical Insurance (Medicare). Not only would the coverage of the state-administered systems involve the analysis of widely varying patterns and experience but, it is believed, it would afford minimal help in defining a consistent and constructive philosophy of social security in America. The author has, therefore, followed the common usage of the American people in terming the combined OASDI and Medicare programs "social security."

In reviewing the historical development of the programs covered, the author has drawn heavily on his extensive personal files as a member of the old age security staff of the Committee on Economic Security in the critical years of 1934 and 1935; as chairman of the Advisory Council on Social Security in 1937-38; and as a member of the four succeeding Advisory Councils, including that of 1969-71. Involvement in the development of social insurance policy has been a part of his lifelong study and activity as an economist specializing in industrial relations and the development of human resources. The judgments on policy are, of course, the author's own, tempered by forty years of discussion with those responsible for or concerned in social security developments.

In order to assist the reader in his further study of history and policy in the field of social security, a carefully selected reading list of significant books and reports is appended. In a controversial area, the points of view of other deeply involved persons help greatly in the process of forming one's own judgment. In a field burdened with complex details of fact or legislation, the official reports will furnish all the material one cares to absorb.

Since revisions in the Social Security Act have become

a frequent occurrence, only legislative reports and official manuals can keep up with detailed changes. Shifts in philosophy and basic policy develop more gradually, however. These latter are the concern of the book. While the more important changes under consideration in Congress in 1971 are reviewed in principle in the text, where specific provisions of legislation are outlined, they are those in effect in 1971.

As a Faculty Associate of the Industrial Relations Section of Princeton University, the author has had the advantage of the incisive comments of Professors Herman M. Somers and Michael K. Taussig, his associates in the Section. He has also benefited greatly by the excellent secretarial services provided by Mrs. Dorothy Silvester, the Administrative Assistant of the Section, and by the expert bibliographical support of Miss Helen Fairbanks, the Librarian of the Section. The author's debt to the officers and staff of the Social Security Administration is likewise great. Not only have they provided the opportunity for numberless discussions of policy over the years, but they have been most generous in helping the author to avoid errors of fact in the difficult task of summarizing in brief compass a complex and evolving body of legislation.

J. DOUGLAS BROWN

*Princeton University*
*September, 1971*

# TABLE OF CONTENTS

ix

CONTENTS

x

An American Philosophy of Social Security

CHAPTER I

# The Genesis of Social Security in America: An Intimate Account of a Critical Period, 1934-35

SOCIAL SECURITY HAS NOW BECOME a common and comforting *expression* in the American language. More important, it has become a meaningful *factor* in meeting the contingencies of life for nine out of ten Americans. In 1934, this vast enterprise in preventing hardship and dependency was but a tenuous idea in the minds of a few deeply concerned individuals. Seldom in modern times has an idea, hammered out by a small group of planners, become in a single generation such a pervasive and practical part of the way of life of a people. "Social security" is now taken for granted. In September 1934, even the term was unknown.

It is in the nature of human aspirations that progress in their fulfillment is measured from one's current state to that desired in the future. Progress in the past becomes merged into the existing way of life and wants are more keenly felt than satisfactions. In the later months of 1971, the newspapers carried numerous reports on proposals for improved family assistance, for national health insurance, and for federal financing of the mounting relief expenditures in our larger cities. A White House conference has focused attention on the unfilled needs of the aged. The term "income maintenance" has become an accepted part of our political vocabulary even though its precise meaning is often vague.

3

The recession of the early 1970's may have been mild in comparison with those which America has repeatedly experienced but it has reinforced anew the persistent conviction of our people that poverty, wherever or whenever it occurs, is inconsistent with the assumed goals of the American people. While in absolute terms the extent of poverty in the United States today is far less than that existing four decades ago and of a different order of magnitude compared to that normal in vast areas of the world, the American citizen, whether poor or rich, is not satisfied with such comparisons, but demands measures for the further elimination of human insecurity.

The goal of universal social security in America reflects the idealism of our people as well as their sensitivity to the dangers of wide differences in personal income in a democratic country. The desirability of the end sought cannot be challenged. It is the means of attaining that end which must concern the leaders of the country. Poverty is probably the most complex and amorphous concept in social economics. The means of preventing it are likewise complex but they cannot be amorphous. Effective measures can be developed if intelligence, understanding, and persistent dedication are marshaled. But these ingredients do not come by any political magic. They must find their source in our past experience and in the faith that past accomplishments can give us.

It is for these reasons that the long and successful development of a great system of poverty prevention, the program now called "social security" by our people, is worthy of review at this time. Those who do not understand history are doomed to repeat its mistakes. They may also miss the opportunity to repeat its successes.

4

The winter of 1932-33 had been a desperate time for millions of Americans. On his inauguration in March, 1933, President Roosevelt set in motion a series of emergency programs to stimulate business recovery, to avoid widespread bank failures, and to alleviate destitution and distress among the unemployed. It was a time for immediate action aimed at quick results. Many of the measures were rough and ready, but the stakes were high in lifting the American people out of the discouragement and hardships of a great depression.

By late spring in 1934, the various emergency measures in support of business and employment were beginning to have their effect. On June 8, 1934, the President sent to Congress a special message giving notice that in January 1935 he would present for its consideration a series of proposals intended to ward off in future years the corroding insecurity which economic collapse had made evident. The time was ripe for more positive and systematic programs for the *prevention* of poverty than the American people would have thought necessary five years before. Just as drastic *emergency* measures had proved acceptable in a period of deep discouragement, it was the President's hope that drastic *constructive* measures for the protection of our people against the hazards of unemployment, old age, and ill health would also be approved. It was important, however, that action be sought as soon as possible before the lessons of the depression began to fade. The President's sense of timing was astute. The difficult task was to plan the constructive, long-run programs in the short time available.

Just as the receding tide makes visible the hidden rocks and reefs that cause disaster, so the great depression of

5

the early 1930's had brought clearly to light the mounting human problems of dependent old age in an industrial, urban economy. The inherent security of life on the farm had become but a romantic memory for the majority of Americans. Dependence on the earnings of grown children was a partial substitute as long as those earnings continued. With widespread unemployment, even this substitute disappeared for many. With the lay-off of a working son, three generations of the family faced increasing poverty. In the cities and industrial towns, there was need to pay rent and buy food and little chance for old people to find work. The loss of savings through bank failures and depreciated investments had reduced many self-reliant old people to dependence on relief.

By 1934, the insecurity of the aged was becoming a distinct and persistent theme within the general clamor for action against mounting hardship. Among many other campaigns for radical remedies for the plight of the aged, the Townsend movement was becoming the most effective. Started in California, where many old people had sought a pleasant and inexpensive place to live, the movement found ready response throughout the country. Especially in the rural areas, such as northern New England and the Middle West, where older people had been left behind as young people moved to the cities, the evangelical appeal of Dr. Townsend and the impossible miracle of his plan for $200 a month gained vigorous support. The supporters were normally conservative people who, in their deepening anxiety, accepted an alluring gospel of economic salvation.

It is difficult, thirty-five years later, to understand the effectiveness of the Townsend movement in exerting pressure on Congress. The scheme of supporting a $200 monthly grant to all people over 65 out of the proceeds of a greatly stimulated business activity caused by their expenditures was an extreme and faulty oversimplification of the function of money in a complex economy. But the compelling appeal was emotional, not economic. At the appeal's height, the supporters of the plan sent millions of postcards to their representatives in Congress. The most effective piece was a simple card depicting two scenes. One showed a forlorn old couple trudging up a snowy road with their few belongings. Underneath was the title, "Over the Hill to the Poorhouse." The other picture showed the same couple seated before a cheery fire, the old lady knitting and the old man smoking his pipe. Its title was "Comfort in Old Age." Across the bottom of the card was the clear-cut message, "Vote for the Townsend Plan."

It was against this background that a number of us were called to Washington in August, 1934, to help produce the constructive proposals for the prevention of insecurity which President Roosevelt had promised the Congress. On June 29, a Committee on Economic Security had been established by executive order. With Frances Perkins, the Secretary of Labor, as chairman, the Committee consisted of the Secretary of the Treasury, the Attorney General, the Secretary of Agriculture, and the Federal Emergency Relief Administrator. Edwin E. Witte of Wisconsin was appointed its executive director. As with similar high-level committees, it was assumed that the major planning effort would be assigned to a staff of specialists assembled for the purpose.

The old age security section of the staff of the Committee on Economic Security was small by comparison to those assigned to unemployment and health insurance. This, however, proved a great boon. Barbara Nachtrieb Armstrong, a professor of law at the University of California, brought as leader of the group a brilliant legal mind, an extensive knowledge of social insurance systems abroad, and an intense concern for human welfare. Her book *Insuring the Essentials* was published in 1932. Murray W. Latimer had a thorough knowledge of industrial pension plans. He and I had worked earlier on a national pension plan for the railroads, and he was the first chairman of the Railroad Retirement Board. I was then Director of the Industrial Relations Section at Princeton University and had served on President Hoover's Emergency Committee for Employment. Otto C. Richter, from the American Telephone and Telegraph Company, assigned to the group as an actuary, took on far broader responsibilities.

On arriving in Washington, we soon found that, despite President Roosevelt's ringing declaration that America should provide protection against *all* the major causes of insecurity, the interest in plans to protect the aged was overshadowed by that in programs to protect the unemployed. This was a natural consequence of the vivid memory we all had of the desperate conditions throughout the country when, a year or two before, thirteen million wage-earners were out of work. It was reinforced, however, by the fact that state programs for unemployment insurance had already been developed in Wisconsin and Ohio. Unemployment insurance had in some way become an "American" idea. Old age insurance was still a foreign and, therefore, a questionable concept.

That the major attention of the Committee on Economic Security and its staff was focused on unemployment insurance proved a great advantage to those of us assigned to planning an old age security program. While vigorous debates ensued on the virtues of the Wisconsin and Ohio approaches, we were left largely alone to work out a national scheme of old age insurance. There were times during the fall of 1934 when the likelihood that a national old age insurance system would be approved by the Committee looked very dim. Ed Witte, as director of the Committee staff, showed little enthusiasm for such a system and appeared to reflect the doubts of those in authority.

Our insistence that there was need for a national contributory social insurance program to meet the need of the aged grew out of our study of the steadily rising balance of old people, compared to the working population, in the years ahead. America had become accustomed to thinking of itself as a young nation, but already the combined factors of longevity, industrialization, and urbanization were making inevitable a serious problem of support for increasing millions of people beyond 65. To attempt to meet the problem by state old age assistance programs alone offered little hope. A more constructive mechanism which would *prevent* a vast load of dependency among the aged was vitally necessary. The only such mechanism available was compulsory contributory old age insurance.

Among a series of memoranda which Barbara Armstrong and I exchanged for criticism in those hectic days, and which I now have in my files, is a much-edited draft that was retyped with the date of September 13, 1934. It

9

is entitled "Plan for Federal Compulsory Contributory Pension Insurance." My file copy is a carbon. The original of this, the first rough draft of an old age insurance plan for the United States, may be lost somewhere in the vast archives in Washington. It bears the marks of being a joint effort by the two of us in trying to create a constructive mechanism to bring the vast and growing problem of old age security under some degree of control.

The purpose of the September 13 plan is stated to be: "To afford assured income to workers 65 and over for the remainder of their lives." From the very first, as evidenced by this early document, it was our conviction that any old age insurance plan in the United States should be *national, compulsory,* and *contributory,* and provide benefits as a *matter of right.* To us, these necessary elements were obvious and came out of a kind of intuitive judgment based on deep hunches on what would work. The retirement age of 65 was, probably, a simple acceptance of an age which had become normal for retirement under American industrial pension plans. I can remember no suggestion of another age.

While convinced from the first that only an integrated, national system of old age insurance would be effective, our chief worry was: Did the federal government have the constitutional authority to impose such a system on the citizens of the United States? In 1934, there was little in the long evolution of American constitutional doctrine to justify an affirmative response.

The problem of constitutionality led us to consider all possible alternatives in the organization and development of a national system. A memorandum by Barbara Armstrong dated September 12 outlined eight possible arrangements. The September 13 plan used a combination of these arrangements which was so cumbersome, ineffective, and actuarially unsound that no further attempt was made to produce a jerry-built scheme in order to avoid a head-on constitutional test of a truly workable system.

A summary of the organizational features of the September 13 plan makes clear in retrospect the inadequacy of clever devices in building a sound social insurance system. The plan proposed that insurance contributions would be required "of all eligible employed workers and their employers in those states and industrial groups electing to come under the scheme." The contributions would be accumulated in a federal pension insurance fund, invested in federal securities, and repaid to the insured person in the form of a pension for life on attainment of age 65. In order to extend the coverage of the federal insurance scheme, it proposed that the states would elect to bring all their eligible workers under compulsory national coverage and that industry groups engaged in interstate commerce could, by a joint agreement of employers and employees, elect compulsory coverage. To encourage states and industry groups to come under coverage, the plan proposed that the federal government provide a supplementary pension to all persons qualifying for the basic pension payments under the scheme.

As a further stimulus to elected coverage by employers, we added for good measure a "shotgun wedding" device which our colleagues working on unemployment insurance programs were finding attractive. This was a payroll tax to be levied on all wages paid to eligible employees by employers engaged in interstate commerce with the

11

proviso that all sums paid as contributions by such employers to the federal pension insurance system be credited against their tax payments.

One shudders to think what the present social security system would be today if any such combination of state and industry election, encouraged by both subsidies and tax incentives, had received any further consideration. If frozen into law, the idea would have resulted in a monstrous patchwork of coverage, with impossible problems of assuring adequate and equitable benefits, actuarial and financial stability, or progressive improvement.

With the firm conviction that there was no alternative to a fully integrated national old age insurance system, we sought the advice of the country's best scholars in constitutional law in seeking ways to give such a system a reasonable chance to survive attack on constitutional grounds. We received valuable help from Professor Thomas Reed Powell of Harvard, Professor Dudley O. McGovney of the University of California, Professor Edwin S. Corwin of Princeton, and Professor Douglas B. Maggs of Duke. Powell, especially, came to our aid when constitutional objections within the staff seemed to block the way.

A dated memorandum indicates that by November 9, 1934, our staff and our academic advisers, as well as Alexander Holtzoff, the assistant to the Attorney General, were convinced that a bold approach in basing the system on the taxing and appropriation powers of the federal government was safer than any indirect taxing device for putting pressure on the states or on industry groups to come under a nationally developed program. Our staff recommendation of that date was clear-cut. It read: "It is recommended that . . . contributory old age insurance, resting on the federal taxing power, be instituted on a national scale, covering all workers for whom it can be practically administered. . . ." This was a critical turning point in the development of social security legislation in this country. It was, however, the beginning of a long battle, not the end.

The position to which we had now come is summarized in a preliminary draft of the official report on the work of the old age security staff:

> In its consideration of the advantages of old age insurance, the staff is fully aware of the limitations imposed upon the Federal Government by our Constitution which would affect the adoption of such a program. The staff is convinced, however, that it should first seek out the most constructive proposals for old age security adapted to American economic and social conditions and then, and only then, test as far as possible whether such proposals can be made effective within our legal system. Since law is a living science, it is reasonable to assume that if a sound program of old age security can be projected, our system of constitutional law will evolve in time to support that program. In the meantime, adjustments may be necessary to mold such a program to existing legal precedents.

It is significant that the more cautious editors of the *printed* version of our report struck out this passage for fear of adverse use. It is far more significant that by 1937, under the leadership of Justice Cardozo, the United States Supreme Court *did* demonstrate that American constitutional law is a living science. Our staff, with the help of the best legal minds in the country, had found a formula which would, if needed, permit the Court to move with the changing concerns of the American people.

The firm conviction of our little group in the old age section of the staff of the Committee on Economic Security that an old age insurance system should be completely *national* was not shared by our colleagues concerned with unemployment insurance. The Wisconsin unemployment insurance plan had strong supporters within the Committee staff. The protection of workers was, by long tradition in America, a function of the several states. We were, therefore, not only facing the precedents of the Supreme Court of the United States, but the predispositions of our immediate colleagues. To convince them of the soundness of our position required awesome descriptions of the complexities of forty-eight separate old age insurance systems.

Suppose, we would postulate, a wage earner developed earnings credits during his working years under the old age insurance schemes of a dozen states. Would he, on retiring, need to cash the checks he received from twelve state funds each month to have enough to pay his bills? Further, how, short of requiring *full* reserves under each state system, could a worker be sure that his benefit would be paid many years later? Full reserves for forty-eight state systems would accumulate to a vast total sum which would far exceed the federal securities available for investment. Could the states be trusted to invest pension funds in their own securities? Would not the effect of the vast accumulation of reserves be deflationary, on the one hand, and an encouragement to unwise and uneven liberality, on the other? How would a single state be able to estimate its pension liability years in advance, given the mobility of the American wage earner and the constant shift in age distribution? Would the estimates for Vermont, California, Mississippi, or Florida bear any semblance of what developed forty years later in terms of contribution-benefit balance? Even *exact* estimates would result in diverse ratios. In the absence of much study of old age insurance on the part of our opponents, our lurid picture of forty-eight diverse state systems usually closed the debate. For good measure, we argued that unemployment insurance should *also* be established on a completely national basis. The slow and spotty progress of unemployment insurance over the years has, I am convinced, fully justified our counter-argument.

During the months from September to December, 1934, Barbara Armstrong, Murray Latimer, Otto Richter, and I hammered away at shaping an old age insurance system appropriate for the United States. There were repeated conferences within the staff of the Committee, with a Technical Board of governmental officers chaired by Arthur J. Altmeyer, with a representative Advisory Council chaired by Frank P. Graham, and with many other interested and qualified persons. In a meeting on November 15, 1934, our ideas were reviewed by Abraham Epstein, long a leader in promoting old age security, and by I. M. Rubinow, whose book *The Quest for Security*, published in 1934, had aroused the interest of President Roosevelt. The day before, the Committee on Economic Security had staged a national conference at the Mayflower Hotel with a reception at the White House. The printed program of the conference lists unemployment insurance, but makes no mention of old age insurance. The latter was still a doubtful starter in the minds of those in authority.

It does not take long for the academic scholar caught up in the vast machinery of national government to realize that a good idea needs public attention to find its way to realization. To give momentum to his campaign for economic security, President Roosevelt used the occasion of the November 14 Conference to address the nation concerning his plans. The substance of the address, as customary, was prepared by the Executive Director and the Chairman of the Committee on Economic Security. Since neither Ed Witte nor Secretary Perkins had the zeal for old age insurance which had by now possessed our staff group, the President's address focused on unemployment insurance and played down the early likelihood of any old age security program: "I do not know whether this is the time for any federal legislation on old age security."

Our staff group was so distressed by this setback that we took desperate measures. Through Max Stern, a friend of Barbara Armstrong in the Scripps-Howard newspaper chain, our concern found its way into a sharply written editorial criticizing the President's failure to give his wholehearted support to old age insurance. Louis Stark in a lead article in the *New York Times* strongly emphasized the general letdown. By the time the newspapers reached Warm Springs, where the President had gone for the weekend, the telephone wires to Secretary Perkins became hot. The Secretary soon communicated the President's displeasure to Ed Witte, who in turn hurried to the office which Barbara Armstrong and

I shared. Much excited, he asked us if we knew how and why the speech has received such a bad press. From then on, the President seemed to take a greater interest in old age insurance. Ed Witte, as a longtime professional in government, was always a bit dismayed by the free-wheeling tactics of the academics on his old age security staff. Somehow, we were more influenced by our own convictions than by the decisions of those in authority.

Apart from that of determining a constitutional basis for a national compulsory old age insurance program, the stickiest problem we faced was finding a workable plan for financing the system over the decades ahead. It was here that our actuarial colleagues, Otto C. Richter and Robert J. Myers, served valiantly in developing a complex series of financial projections and in making clear the alternatives faced. Richter and Latimer brought to bear their thorough knowledge of industrial annuity programs. To pay even reasonably modest benefits to those already approaching retirement required the assumption by the system of a heavy accrued liability. While current contributions would be fully sufficient to meet these early benefits, how far should this accrued liability be recognized by the gradual building of reserves to meet it when younger contributors became eligible for their benefits? In private individual insurance, a full reserve would be considered essential. Even in group annuity programs set up by private firms, accrued liability had to be funded over time. In social insurance, however, we were convinced that such a full reserve was not only unnecessary, but an impossible incubus on the national economy. Not only would the accumulation of the reserve be deflationary and a temptation

17

to unwise use, but, in 1934, there was no prospect that there would be enough federal securities in which to invest it. In place of a large reserve, we were convinced, an eventual government contribution to the system would be necessary.

By November 9, according to an "Outline of Old Age Security Program Proposed by Staff," we had come to realize that a compromise between a "pay-as-you-go" plan of financing and a reserve plan was necessary. By November 16, a formal staff report indicated, with some diplomatic subtlety, that an advisory actuarial board and the representatives of the Treasury "have combined to convince [sic] the staff that a straight reserve system is out of the question because of the enormous reserves it would involve." It warned, however, that "a predominantly pay-as-you-go scheme entails the disadvantage of sudden large and increasing contributions from the government about 25 years from the date of initiating the insurance." The compromise plan we proposed provided for a gradually increasing contribution rate starting at ½ of 1 percent and reaching 2½ percent each on employers and employees by 1956. The federal government was called upon to contribute an amount sufficient to maintain an eleven-billion-dollar reserve once this was attained.

The provision for an eventual government subsidy to the system seemed to us to be the only possible way of paying reasonable benefits in the early years, and, at the same time, of avoiding a huge invested reserve. In our words at the time, this "should not be a dangerous venture . . . provided the annual pension burdens are

18

anticipated and planned for." With both contribution rates and benefits now far higher than we had ever dreamed, the issue of an eventual governmental subsidy to the system is still unresolved.

There were many other problems to be solved in those hectic months in the fall and early winter of 1934-35. In error, we followed European precedent in proposing the exemption from coverage of nonmanual workers earning in excess of $50 a week. Congress, fortunately, was wiser in covering the first segment of earnings regardless of the occupation of the employee. Departing from European tradition, we proposed the use of a uniform percentage of wages in determining the amount of contribution rather than a flat dollar amount or a series of amounts by wage classes. Our reason was the need to adapt the social insurance system to the wide range of wage levels throughout the United States and to American accounting procedures. The decision, which seemed obvious at the time, has resulted in far greater advantages in the development and administration of the system than we could then realize.

In that pre-electronic age, the best idea we could suggest to assure full collection of insurance contributions was to use special revenue stamps. A British stamp book which I displayed before the House Ways and Means Committee in January so intrigued the members that they ordered that it be reproduced in the official record of the hearings, where it can be seen today. Despite the awe-inspiring complications of such a collection system, as one looks back, I still feel that my learned explanation of its use made an insurance system seem more feasible

19

to congressmen in 1935. In selling an automobile, an understandable gadget may have more appeal than the design of a motor.

From the first, we assumed that contributions to old age insurance should be "in equal shares by employer and insured employee" as stated in the September 13 draft. A "fifty-fifty" ratio seemed to us to be justified by an "aesthetic" logic difficult to contravert. There never was any objection from the labor movement against equal contributions to old age insurance.

Our early ideas on benefit structure were necessarily tentative. It was the Advisory Council on Social Security in 1937-38 which developed the basic pattern of benefits which is now incorporated in the system. Our report to the Committee on Economic Security in December 1934, proposed "a larger relative annuity for lower-paid workers by weighting more heavily the first $15 of weekly wage." Weekly benefits were to start after the system had been in operation for 5 years and after 200 weeks of contributions by an individual. They were to be a modest minimum percent of average covered wages, supplemented by a percent of average wages related to years of coverage. We were so anxious to keep within the financial limitations then assumed necessary that the maximum weekly benefit for persons then employed would have been but $14.00 *after 20 years of coverage*! It must be remembered that the maximum old age assistance grant contemplated at the time was less than $7.50 a week. Also, the contribution rate proposed was, at the start, but one-half a percent each on employer and employee up to a maximum coverage of $35 a week.

Our staff group may have been radical in proposing a

national social insurance system, but it could not have been accused of financial irresponsibility in proposing fancy benefits. While quite inadequate and too long delayed, the benefits then proposed were far less important strategically, we were convinced, than the establishment of the principle of old age benefits as a *matter of right*, related to past contributions to a national system. Three years later, with constitutionality assured, and a far greater opportunity to study the complex financial and actuarial aspects of the system, the Advisory Council of 1937-38 was able to take advantage of a higher contribution rate to provide for far more adequate benefits without the long delay we thought to be necessary. In December 1934, time was short, Congress was about to assemble, and a bill had to be drafted or we would miss the boat. Our desperate hope was to get a compulsory contributory national system of old age insurance through Congress. We assumed that no benefits would be paid for five years and this would give our successors plenty of time to work out a better benefit structure.

The likelihood of gaining the support of the Cabinet Committee for our proposals was still in doubt. At this critical time, December, 1934, help came from an unexpected source, the industrial executives on the Committee's Advisory Council. Fortunately included in the Council were Walter C. Teagle of the Standard Oil Company of New Jersey, Gerard Swope of General Electric, and Marion Folsom of Eastman Kodak, and others well acquainted with industrial pension plans. Their practical understanding of the need for contributory old age annuities on a broad, national basis carried great weight with those in authority. They enthusiastically approved our

21

program. Just as the newspaper writers had carried us through the November crisis, the support of progressive industrial executives in December ensured that a national system of contributory old age insurance would be recommended to the President and the Congress. Even last minute concerns on the part of Secretary Morgenthau and President Roosevelt on the financing of the system failed to reverse the momentum gained. By this time, the Townsend pressure for an impossible panacea for the problems of old age security was encouraging belated interest in a constructive contributory insurance system.

For some of us, the submission of our staff recommendations was the beginning and not the end of association with the development of the American social security system. Appearance in congressional hearings, participation in committee executive sessions, and many conferences on strategy were interspersed with weeks of anxious waiting. Barbara Armstrong and I had earlier explained the proposed old age insurance plan to Senator Wagner, who supported it valiantly. Outside of Washington, hard work was necessary to convince industrial executives, generally, of the soundness of a single contributory national plan which could become a solid uniform floor for private *supplementary* pension plans in contrast to any arrangement for "contracting out" from coverage.

On August 14, 1935, the Social Security Act became law. The next step was to assure its constitutionality. It was a rewarding experience to help Charles E. Wyzanski, Jr., who presented the case for the government. There was need also to help both the new Social Security Board and the Treasury in getting the program under way. On May 24, 1937, Justice Cardozo delivered the decision of the Supreme Court sustaining the old age insurance parts of the Act.

In the same month, an Advisory Council on Social Security was appointed. At the suggestion of Gerard Swope, I was elected Chairman of the Council. The Social Security Board was now a going concern and had both staff and time to think out problems which were left unsolved in the fall of 1934. After more than a year of study, the twenty-five-member Advisory Council hammered out a benefit structure which provided, in addition to basic pensions, protection for wives, widows, and surviving children starting in 1940. Our staff report had, in 1934, indicated the inevitability of this step. The Council of 1937-38 also approved, in principle, disability benefits, and established basic guidelines on coverage and financing, including that of an eventual government contribution to the system as recommended by our staff.

To one who has participated in the planning of the social security system since its inception, the most remarkable outcome over the years is the degree to which fundamental concepts, hammered out in 1934, have guided the development of one of the largest ventures in social engineering in the world. The system remains, basically, national, compulsory, and contributory. Benefits are a matter of right. Coverage is almost universal for workers outside of government. Contributions are a percentage of wages, with equal shares paid by employer and employee. A pay-as-you-go plan of financing is coupled with a limited contingency reserve invested in federal securities. It is in a greatly improved benefit structure that the system has moved farthest from the limited proposals of our small staff in 1934. Even if time had

23

then been available, I doubt that we could have anticipated what experience has shown to be feasible in building a more adequate social security system.

In 1934, the American people greatly needed a constructive program for the prevention of poverty in old age. The experience of the depression prepared the way for a drastic new step. A great President, when convinced of the feasibility of the program, was ready to take bold advantage of a uniquely favorable political situation to push through legislation. The need was for a workable plan which matched the predispositions of the American people, if not the constitutional precedents of the country. In a few short months, a plan was developed, based upon *ideas* rather than on vast statistical studies or extensive scientific research. Those ideas, tested over a third of a century, have proved to be sound and acceptable as the guidelines of a vast enterprise in the enhancement of the welfare of a people.

## CHAPTER II

# The American Social Security Program Today

EVEN TO THOSE WHO HAVE been closely concerned in the development of the American social security program since its beginnings in 1934, the present size and scope of the program's operations seem too vast to have been the result of the ideas and efforts described in the last chapter. A closely interlocked system of protection in old age, survivorship, disability and sickness, touching the lives of practically every family in the United States, has grown out of the limited and hurriedly designed version of old age insurance planned and enacted in the hectic months from September 1934 to August 1935. Now nine out of every ten people in paid employment or self-employment are covered or are eligible for coverage under the program. About 91 percent of the elderly are either getting benefits or will be eligible for them when they or their spouses retire. Of those reaching 65 in 1971, 93 percent are eligible for benefits. Ninety-five out of every one hundred children under 18, as well as their mothers, can count on monthly cash benefits if the family breadwinner should die. In total, more than 26 million men, women, and children, one out of every eight in the country, are getting monthly cash benefits.

The hospital insurance program now protects almost all of the 20,500,000 persons over 65, and the medical insurance program almost as many. Medicare payments now cover two-thirds of the expenditures for hospital and physicians' services provided to the aged. In July 1971, monthly cash benefits under Old Age, Survivors and Disability Insurance (OASDI) were $2,984,000,000, at an annual rate of over thirty-five billion. Hospital services compensated, in July 1971, totaled $477,300,000, and physicians' and other services, $169,900,000.

While these figures are most impressive, they are far less helpful in a study of the philosophy of social security policy than a brief summary of just what the system has come to mean for the typical beneficiary or potential beneficiary. A complete explanation of eligibility requirements and benefit amounts would require a sizeable handbook. A clearer picture can be gained, it is believed, by presenting a series of quite usual situations where protection is provided.

The simplest case is that of a single man, "Mr. Jones," retiring completely in 1971 at age 65 after long coverage under the OASDI program. He is eligible for old age insurance benefits because his record shows that he has earned at least $50 in covered employment for at least one-fourth of the eighty three-month periods since 1951, or the equivalent of five years out of twenty completed years. To compute his benefit amount, called for purposes of this book a "primary benefit," his covered earnings, year by year, are averaged over fifteen of the twenty completed years before 1971. (His five years of lowest earnings are dropped.) Assuming that this average of his best fifteen years is $4,800, or $400 a month, his monthly benefit will be $194.40 a month.

If Mr. Jones, because of loss of job, or for any other reason except total disability, had decided to retire at age 62, the computation of his average covered wages would be affected to some degree since three of what ordinarily would be his five drop-out years of low earnings would have to be used in figuring his average earnings in order to eliminate from his average the years of no work from 62 to 65. Even if his average wage remained $4,800 a year, he would face a reduction in the primary benefit to $155.60 a month to offset the actuarial cost of providing him with three additional years of benefit during his retirement. This is to assure that the cost to the system will not be increased by his early retirement.

On the other hand, if he is regularly employed, Mr. Jones might decide to postpone his retirement until age 67. Since the computation of average covered wages uses as a base only the span of years up to the full year before age 65, regardless of later retirement, Mr. Jones would then have the advantage of having two additional years from which the best fifteen are taken to determine his average wages. Since American wages have risen steadily since the mid-1950's and the statutory maximum on covered wages has been raised repeatedly since then, it is very likely that the two additional years, substituting for those in the mid-1950's, will improve his average and therefore his monthly benefit.

A more typical case would be that Mr. Jones retired on benefit at either 65 or 62 and, thereafter, supplemented his benefit by part-time work. Under the legislation in effect in 1971, his benefit would be unaffected by annual earnings up to $1,680. Beyond that amount, he would lose one dollar of benefit for each two dollars earned up to $2,880. Beyond $2,880, he would lose one dollar in benefit for each dollar earned. This arrangement, called the "earnings test," will probably be changed because of mounting objection to so complex an arrangement. The recommendation of the 1969-71 Advisory

Council is that the first $2,000 in earnings have no effect on benefits and that the offset above that be one dollar of benefit for each two dollars of earnings until the whole benefit is eliminated.

If Mr. Jones is married and his wife is 65 when Mr. Jones starts getting benefits, she will receive 50 percent of his benefit, or $97.20. If she is at least 62, but not yet 65, the monthly amount will be reduced to bring her total payments for life to the same total on an actuarial basis as if her benefits had begun at age 65.

Mrs. Jones may, however, have had sufficient covered earnings since 1937 to make her eligible for a benefit larger than 50 percent of her husband's primary benefit. In this case she will automatically receive her own higher benefit amount. Should Mr. Jones die after Mrs. Jones has reached 62, she will receive as a widow's benefit an amount equivalent to 82½ percent of Mr. Jones' benefit, or $160.40 a month. If Mr. Jones had died earlier, his widow could have claimed her widow's benefit at age 60 at an actuarially reduced rate of $139.10 a month.

If, in the reverse of the more usual situation, Mr. Jones were an invalid dependent on Mrs. Jones, her earnings would be the basis for a retirement benefit for herself, with an allowance for Mr. Jones of 50 percent. Should Mrs. Jones die, Mr. Jones' dependent widower's benefit would be 82½ percent of his wife's benefit.

There are still other possible contingencies facing the Jones family which need to be considered as they approach old age. Perhaps, because of a late marriage, they have a child under 18 when Mr. Jones claims his benefit at age 65, or a child 18 to 21 attending school full time.

A benefit of 50 percent, or $97.20 a month, otherwise payable on behalf of the child, based on Mr. Jones' benefit of $194.40, would be limited to $63.20 on account of the family maximum limit of $354.70 related to his benefit amount. However, $145.80 would be paid in addition to the widow's benefit if Mr. Jones should die while the child is under 18, or under 22, if in school.

Perhaps, on the other hand, Mr. Jones has neither a wife nor children, but is supporting a dependent parent when he retires or dies. Subject to the family maximum amount indicated, a surviving dependent aged parent would receive 82½ percent of Jones' benefit, or $160.40 a month; two such parents would receive 75 percent each.

In this way, protection based on Mr. Jones' earnings might extend to three generations, his parents, his wife, and his children, although, usually, at the time of a man's retirement, only his wife is dependent upon him for support. Social insurance cannot, however, cover only the usual situations, but must, within reasonable limits, as established by the family maximum amount, anticipate the many variations which exist in the interdependent family unit.

Shifting to the contingencies faced by a younger family, there are again many possible situations which the social security program now covers. For illustration, Mr. and Mrs. Smith have three children aged 12, 10, and 8. Mr. Smith is 37 and has been earning a good salary since graduation from college. Mrs. Smith worked before marriage and returned to work as a secretary as soon as her children were in school. In 1971, Mr. Smith is killed in

29

an automobile accident. Regardless of other insurance or savings, the Smith family is protected by OASDI to the following extent.

Using Mr. Smith's yearly covered earnings, beginning with 1956, the year after he was 21, and dropping out his five years of lowest earnings, his average covered earnings for his ten best years before 1971 is, let us assume, $6,000, approximately the maximum possible for this period of coverage under OASDI. Based on this record, the benefits payable to the Smith family are among the highest afforded by the system. Whether or not Mrs. Smith discontinues work to take care of her three children, the total benefit payable will be $412.30 a month, the family maximum payable on her husband's primary benefit of $224.70. Each survivor is entitled to a benefit equal to 75 percent of the husband's benefit for a total of $673.60 a month, but because of the statutory family maximum of $412.30 related to Mr. Smith's benefit, the benefit of each of the four survivors would be reduced to bring the total within the maximum applied to the family. The benefit of $412.30 will continue as long as at least three survivors are getting benefits. When only two survivors are being paid the amount drops to $337.20 a month. When the youngest child reaches 18, Mrs. Smith's benefit, to which she is entitled as a widowed mother, ceases. The benefits for the children, if they are in school or college and remain unmarried, could continue until they become 22, subject always, however, to the family maximum. If the family maximum would otherwise be exceeded at any time, the shares to the children, if they are still eligible, would be prorated among them to come within maximum allowed.

30

There are two additional contingencies which may affect the Smith family following the death of Mr. Smith. If one of the children has a continuing, serious disability, such as mental retardation, protection for the child will not terminate at age 18 or 22, and protection for the mother will continue so long as the child is under her care. Also, if Mrs. Smith does not remarry or become entitled to a benefit in her own right which exceeds that of a widow's benefit based on her deceased husband's benefit, she will receive that widow's benefit in her old age. At age 62, this would be $185.40 a month; at age 60, $160.70 a month.

In the foregoing illustration, it was postulated that Mrs. Smith was well able to make considerable earnings as a secretary. After the death of her husband, it is natural for her to seek at least part-time work to help meet the family's needs. Regardless of how high her earnings are, the full family benefit of $412.30 would be payable because under the earnings test only her own benefits are reduced because of her earnings and each of the three children is entitled to $168.40, subject to the family limitation of $412.30. When only two or three survivors are entitled to benefits, Mrs. Smith may wish to limit the amount of work she does because her earnings can then affect the amount of the total benefits payable to the family. For example, when only Mrs. Smith and one child are on the rolls, they will each get a benefit of $168.40. If Mrs. Smith works and earns, under the 1971 rules, $1,680 in a year, her benefits will not be affected. However, for earnings from $1,680 to $2,880, her benefit will be reduced by one dollar for each two dollars earned and, above $2,880, by one dollar for each dollar earned.

Any probable earnings beyond $2,880 a year will afford the family no net advantage and may result in loss because of the expenses involved in going to work and in securing help while Mrs. Smith is away from home.

A different contingency faced by the Smith family would be that Mrs. Smith, instead of her husband, was killed in the automobile accident. If she had worked before and during marriage sufficiently to be eligible for at least a minimum primary benefit, her children, but not her husband, would be eligible for survivors' benefits. Her *level* of earnings when working and her *average* earnings, as affected by periods when not employed, would probably provide but a modest primary benefit. But even if her computed average earnings were but $100 a month, a single eligible child would receive $70.40 a month, two or three eligible children together would get $135.90 a month, the family maximum based on her benefit amount of $90.60. Their continuing eligibility would be under the same limitations as those outlined in the case of the father's death. Since the benefits are related to the mother's earnings, the father's earnings would not affect them. If he also died, the higher benefits related to the father's primary benefit would be substituted. The fact that a working mother now provides, on her death, survivorship protection for her children, even if her husband is living and employed, is often overlooked, since the definition of dependency which makes this possible was changed as recently as 1967.

In the foregoing cases, on the death of the insured person, Mr. Jones, Mr. Smith, or Mrs. Smith, all of whom are eligible through their own earnings records, a lump-sum death payment is provided. This is equivalent to three times the primary benefit amount with a maximum of $255. Since the eligible survivors are otherwise protected, this death payment is assumed to help provide for burial or other final expenses. It is payable to a widow or widower, or, if these do not survive, to the person who paid the burial expenses, or to the funeral home if the funeral expenses are not otherwise paid. The amount has purposely been kept minimal over the years to avoid undue diversion of funds from the more urgent need to protect survivors.

To illustrate the protection afforded by the disability provisions of the OASDI system, we can return to the Smith family. Instead of dying as a result of his unfortunate automobile accident, Mr. Smith is so seriously disabled that he cannot be expected to engage in any substantial gainful activity for at least a year and probably for the remainder of his life. After a waiting period of six months, his benefit of $224.70 a month becomes payable. Since his wife has children under her care, she will be entitled to a wife's benefit of $112.40 and each child will be entitled to a child's benefit of $112.40. Because the family maximum payable on Mr. Smith's benefit is $412.30, the amounts payable to the dependents will be reduced to $46.90 each. Assuming that Mr. Smith remains disabled, the total of $412.30 will continue for the ten years until the youngest child becomes eighteen. At that time, Mrs. Smith's benefit will terminate. Mr. Smith's benefit will continue. If in school, each child will continue to receive until age 22 a benefit readjusted in amount and subject to the family maximum. When Mr. Smith becomes 65, assuming continuous disablement, the payment will automatically become an old age benefit.

If Mrs. Smith does not develop a larger benefit based on her own earnings, she will be eligible for an aged wife's benefit of $112.40 at age 65 or a reduced benefit of $84.30 at age 62, based on her husband's record.

The case of the Smith family has been postulated to give a sense of the upper range of possible protection to a middle-income American family which meets with disaster. For many families, the husband's primary benefit would be much less, although the graduations in benefit structure favor the lower-paid worker. In May 1971, the average disabled beneficiary's benefit, in current status, was $145.33, not Mr. Smith's $224.70. Newly awarded disability benefits had, however, risen to an average of $154.62. The primary benefit we assigned to Mr. Jones of $194.40 a month compares to an average of new awards for retired workers in May 1971, of $133.77.

With this caveat, however, it is interesting to make a rough approximation of the amount of protection afforded the Smith family as a not too exceptional case. As long as the family receives the family maximum, which would be approximately ten years in the case of his total disability, this would be $412.30 a month or $4,947.60 a year. This would be approximately 82.5 percent of his average annual *covered* wages for his previous ten best years. It would be nontaxable. Any earnings he may have had above those covered under OASDI, however, would be lost, and his average covered earnings over the ten-year base period could be considerably less than his most recent earnings before disablement. Still, ten years' protection at $4,947.60, or $49,476, is an impressive sum. Added to this would be his continuing disability benefit from age 47 until death, perhaps 25 years later, or 25

34

times $2,696.40 a year, or $67,410. Further added to this might be the brief period of protection of the children while in school from 18 to 22, and, if Mrs. Smith does not become eligible for a higher old age benefit in her own right, her wife's or, later, her aged widow's benefit from age 65 or 62 until death. Thus, without counting the protection afforded the children after 18 or of Mrs. Smith after age 62, the Smith family benefits, under the benefit schedule in effect in 1971, could well amount to approximately $117,000 over a period of thirty-five years. It is a highly significant feature of the OASDI program that this sum is distributed over the years to match as precisely as possible the imputed needs of the family.

The Smith family case must, however, remain hypothetical for many reasons. Benefit structures will continue to change, ideally in close parallel with costs of living. Since the financing of the OASDI system is largely on a current-cost basis, adjustments can be made in contribution flow to keep the purchasing power of benefits from declining, despite the effect of inflation upon what a dollar will buy. But many things can happen to the Smith family, also. Mr. Smith may die later as a result of his accident so that Mrs. Smith's benefit becomes that of a widowed mother with children. Mrs. Smith may then remarry. On the other hand, Mr. Smith may, with the aid of rehabilitation training, recover sufficiently to return to substantial employment or to part-time employment. The parents or the children might earn sufficient amounts to supplement, or to offset, in part or in whole, the benefits assigned on their behalf. The OASDI program must be flexible and sensitive enough to adjust to all these contingencies under equable and reasonable regulations administered with the intent of providing the most adequate protection possible with the funds available to the system.

Since the purpose of outlining the protection afforded the Joneses and the Smiths is to provide a realistic basis for an analysis of the American social security system in terms of philosophy and policy, a host of detailed legal and administrative complications in benefit operations have been passed over.

The cases which have been outlined suggest the main features of the system of cash benefits under the American social security program. Before illustrating the protection now afforded by the health insurance program (Medicare) under the Social Security Act it may be helpful to indicate several basic differences in the operation of OASDI and Medicare. Most basic is the fact that Medicare provides essentially a service benefit—health care —even though in many cases the covered charges of a physician may be reimbursed to the beneficiary in cash. Further, Medicare, as now constituted, covers only persons aged 65 or more. Also, because of a historical, political accident, it is divided into two parts, Part A. Hospital Insurance and Part B. Medical Insurance. Finally, because of the highly decentralized organization of health services throughout the country, the administration of Medicare includes a combination of widely decentralized initiation of claims, processed through a system of regional private insurance carriers acting as agents of the Social Security Administration but, in the final stage, reviewed and financed by the central Administration.

With this background, let us return to the case of Mr. or Mrs. Jones, assuming that both are 65 or over and have enrolled under *Part B* of the Medicare program with premiums deducted from their monthly benefits. In the simplest situation, Mr. Jones, let us assume, suffers from high blood pressure and visits his doctor at his office. The doctor prescribes drugs and charges $7 for an office call. Since Medicare does not pay for the first $50 of physicians' charges in a calendar year, Mr. Jones will pay the $7 bill but will hold the bill to prove later that this much of his deductible of $50 in the calendar year has been met. Because of his condition and because of other ailments, Mr. Jones returns to his doctor repeatedly during the year. After his total bills exceed $50, either he or his doctor initiates a claim to the regional agency representing Medicare. If the total has become $80, and if he has already paid his doctor, he will receive reimbursement of 80 percent of the $30 paid in excess of his $50 deductible, or $24, provided the $80 comes within the limit of "reasonable charges." If his doctor takes assignment of his claim, he will owe his doctor only the $50 for the deductible and $6 for his share of the remaining balance, or a total of $56. The likelihood is that in a series of small bills, Mr. Jones will pay his doctor from time to time and wait until he has accumulated well over $50 in bills, paid or unpaid, before making his claim. His claim is made to the regional carrier serving as agent for the Medicare program. He will receive notification of payments to be made to him or to the doctor on his behalf, of his status in respect to meeting the annual deductible amount, of the amount of coinsurance involved, and of any charge beyond that approved as "reasonable" under the plan.

It would be a marked advantage in the provision of

physicians' services under Part B of Medicare if all physicians participating in the plan accepted as their full charges the "reasonable charges" as determined under Medicare guidelines for each kind of service rendered. In this case, the physician, on "assignment" by the beneficiary, transmits the claim for reimbursement for the amount charged, except for the once-a-year deductible of $50 and 20 percent coinsurance on each charge. These latter amounts would be paid by the beneficiary to the doctor, thereby completing his part of the transaction. However, there is no way for Medicare to require the physician to limit his charge to the "reasonable" charge as determined under Medicare guidelines. If, for example, Mr. Jones' doctor charged $10 for an office call, and Medicare allowed but $7, Mr. Jones would need to present the doctor's bill in his claim and, though paying the doctor $10, receive, after meeting his annual deductible, but 80 percent of $7 or $5.60. It is true, however, that the doctor's office may assist him in transmitting his claim, even though not accepting assignment thereof as previously explained.

Under both Parts A and B of Medicare, unlike OASDI, the procedures involved in providing health protection to Mrs. Jones, once 65 and enrolled, are distinct from, but precisely parallel to, those outlined for Mr. Jones. Since the need for hospital, medical, and other covered services are very much an *individual* need, beneficiaries are considered as individuals in respect to claims, deductibles, coinsurance, or limits under all aspects of Medicare.

To illustrate the protection which the combination of Parts A and B of Medicare affords in more serious contingencies, let us assume that Mrs. Jones falls and incurs a severe fracture of her hip. She is taken to the hospital in an ambulance and, after X-rays and laboratory tests, is operated upon. After ten days in the hospital, she is transferred to an "extended care facility." When sufficiently recovered after two more weeks, she is sent home, but, remaining under the care of her doctor, is visited a number of times by a visiting nurse and a physical therapy specialist who helps her walk again, using appropriate equipment.

On entering the hospital, Mrs. Jones' Medicare account number is registered and from then on Part A of the program provides the following hospital benefits: a. except for a deductible approximating the charge for one day in hospital ($60 in 1971), the full cost of bed and board (in semi-private accommodations unless a private room is medically justified); b. X-ray services; c. regular nursing care (including intensive care nursing if required); d. laboratory tests; e. drugs provided by the hospital; f. operating room charges; g. medical supplies; h. the use of appliances furnished by the hospital.

When Mrs. Jones is transferred to the extended care facility after her recovery from her operation, her semi-private bed and board, her nursing, drugs, physical therapy, supplies, and the use of appliances are provided without any further deductible. Unless she remains more than twenty days, there is no coinsurance. When she comes home, there are provided part-time visiting-nurse services, physical therapy, part-time services of home-health aides, medical supplies, if furnished by the home-health agency, and the use of medical appliances needed to help her learn to walk again. However, other drugs are not provided after she returns home. If Mrs. Jones

39

is slow in recovering from her injury and remains confined to her home, home-health visiting services may continue up to 100 visits within the year following her discharge from the extended care facility, if her doctor so determines at that time.

Meanwhile, during Mrs. Jones' illness, she has received physician's and surgeon's services under *Part B* of Medicare as an enrolled member. (Her premiums have been deducted from her old age insurance benefit over the years.) Under the same arrangements and limitations as in the case of Mr. Jones, including the annual deductible and the 20 percent coinsurance, the *reasonable* charges for these services are met under Part B of Medicare. Laboratory and X-ray services are met without coinsurance if provided by the hospital, even though performed by physicians. In addition, Part B provides for the use of an ambulance where, as in Mrs. Jones' case, this was medically necessary.

Over the whole period of hospital, extended care, and home-health services, Mrs. Jones may be billed only for the *two* deductibles, $60 for the hospital services under Part A and $50 for the medical services under Part B, plus a 20 percent coinsurance charge for the latter. It may be true in some situations that the charges for Mrs. Jones under *Part B* may exceed those scheduled as reasonable by the Medicare plan. The difference, probably limited in amount, will be payable by Mrs. Jones.

In Mrs. Jones' illness, the periods in the hospital and the extended care facility fell well within the limits of full coverage. If her illness had been far more serious and had involved a much longer stay, after 60 days in the hospital she would pay a coinsurance charge of $15 a day for the next 30 days. After 90 days, she would need to draw upon a "lifetime reserve" of 60 additional days with a coinsurance charge of $30 a day. If her stay in the extended care facility went beyond 20 days, she would pay a coinsurance charge of $7.50 for a further 80 days. In the exceptional circumstance that her stays for a continuous illness exceeded these limits, her Medicare protection would terminate.

If Mrs. Jones recovers entirely from her hip injury and she does not become a bed patient in a hospital or extended care facility for at least 60 days, she would start a new "benefit period" and would be eligible again for the full number of days of hospital and extended care service outlined above, except for any use she had made of her life reserve.

There are, of course, many contingencies not covered in the illustrative cases we have chosen. The intention has been to afford a sense of reality to the protection afforded under Medicare. A full analysis of Medicare arrangements, as a service benefit involving a wide range of human ailments, provided by a complex and unstandardized system of health distribution, and administered through highly decentralized units, would be of more concern to students of social insurance administration than those seeking a philosophical basis for social insurance policy. The reader who wants to know what happens in the endless variety of contingencies befalling millions of Americans, from the Aarons to the Zydorskis, is referred to the *Social Security Handbook* provided by the Social Security Administration for a modest charge.

Easier yet, if his own case concerns him, the nearest office of the Administration will be both generous and accurate in explaining his potential benefits under the American system of social security.

## CHAPTER III

# The Process of Implementing a Philosophy: The Role of Advisory Councils, 1937-71

BEFORE ENTERING UPON an analysis of the particular elements of philosophy and policy which have been implemented in the evolving structure of the American social security system, or of other policies which, it is believed, should guide its further growth, it is relevant at this point to outline the special conditions which have surrounded the process of moving from ideas to implementation in this area of government activity. In social planning, as in cooking, the proof of the pudding is in the eating, and there are many recipes in the cookbook which fail to produce expected results. The interplay of theory, policy, and effective implementation is illustrated with exceptional clarity in the history of the American social security program.

In developing a national system of contributory social insurance, the American people and their government embarked upon a complex *cooperative* endeavor. Unlike most other governmental functions, the system is not merely another form of taxes to support general services or benefits. Rather it is a closely integrated mechanism for the creation of individual rights related to individual contributions which partakes of the nature of a private transaction of purchase and sale, on the one hand, but involves, on the other, the exercise and implementation of sovereign powers of compulsion and sensitive social criteria of need. Further, a social security system, inev-

43

itably, is bound to become highly complex. It requires a combination of political, economic, social, and actuarial judgments in adjusting the mechanism to a wide variety of changing needs of the people to be protected, and, at the same time, a weighing of such adjustments with precision against the costs involved.

The complexity of the American social security system will become more and more evident as the particular features are analyzed. It is sufficient for the present to suggest that the planning of the system requires more than the usual machinery of Congress, dealing routinely with the recommendations of an executive department or agency seeking an expanded budget. It is fortunate that in more recent years the Committee on Ways and Means of the House of Representatives, under the able leadership of the Honorable Wilbur D. Mills, has, through long and concentrated attention, developed a high degree of competency in the analysis of social security issues. That Committee, however, is continuously under heavy pressure because of its wide and critical responsibilities for initiating complex fiscal legislation. The Social Security Administration under Commissioner Robert M. Ball and his predecessors has gained great respect through wise leadership and highly competent staffing. But it remains true that our system of government, unlike that of Great Britain, does not assure close and continuing coordination between the leadership of the executive and that of the legislative branch. The development of our social security system has, fortunately, benefited at its more critical stages by the insertion of a small but effective link between these two branches of government.

This link is the *ad hoc* statutory Advisory Council on

44

Social Security. The first Advisory Council of 1937-38 has already been mentioned. It will be referred to repeatedly hereafter since it has had great and continuing influence upon the character of the social security system today. Most of its recommendations have long since become implemented in well-tested elements of the system. Its creation was, however, something of a historical accident and not the result of legislation, as in the case of more recent Councils. Rather, it was an inspired decision on the part of members of the Committee on Finance of the Senate and Arthur Altmeyer, the Chairman of the Social Security Board. All concerned realized the complexity of the task of revising the titles of the Social Security Act of 1935 which had given birth to a new and untried old age insurance program. They agreed that the help of an external, deliberative, and representative body like a British Royal Commission was needed to hammer out the basic philosophy and policy underlying the fundamental revisions that appeared to be needed.

The circumstances of the appointment of the Advisory Council of 1937-38 can be best described by citing the text used in announcing its establishment. The specific terms of reference, outlining the elements of policy to be considered, will be cited from time to time hereafter when these elements of policy are analyzed:

At a hearing before the Committee on Finance of the United States Senate on February 22, 1937, it was agreed that the Chairman of the Committee on Finance would appoint a special committee to cooperate with the Social Security Board to study the advisability of amending Titles II and VIII of the

Social Security Act. The Chairman of the Committee on Finance has appointed such a special committee consisting of Senator Pat Harrison, Senator Harry Flood Byrd, and Senator Arthur H. Vandenberg. It was agreed that this special committee in cooperation with the Social Security Board would appoint an Advisory Council on Social Security to assist in studying the advisability of amending Titles II and VIII of the Social Security Act.

This first Advisory Council consisted of six members representing employees, six representing employers, and thirteen representing the public. Included in the twenty-five was a wide cross-section of experienced executives and recognized specialists. Among the trade union leaders were Sidney Hillman, President of the Amalgamated Clothing Workers; Philip Murray, then Vice President of the United Mine Workers; John Frey, President of the Metal Trades Department of the American Federation of Labor; Harvey Fremming, President of the Oil Workers; Matthew Woll, Vice President of the Photo Engravers and President of the Union Labor Life Insurance Company; and G. M. Bugniazet, Secretary of the Electrical Workers (C.I.O.) and President of the Union Cooperative Insurance Association. Lee Pressman, General Counsel of C.I.O., served as alternate for Mr. Hillman.

The employer members, likewise a very able group, included Marion Folsom, Treasurer of Eastman Kodak, who was later to become Secretary of Health, Education and Welfare; Walter Fuller, President of Curtis Publishing; Jay Iglauer, Vice President and Treasurer of Halle Brothers' department store; Albert Linton, President of

Provident Mutual Life; E. R. Stettinius, Chairman of the Board of United States Steel, later to become Secretary of State; and Gerard Swope, President of General Electric.

Most of the public members were university professors with a special interest in economic and social policy. They included Paul Douglas of the University of Chicago, later U.S. Senator from Illinois; William Haber of the University of Michigan; Alvin Hansen of Harvard; Theresa McMahon of the University of Washington; A. H. Mobray of the University of California at Berkeley; T. L. Norton of the University of Buffalo; George Stocking of the University of Texas; Edwin Witte of the University of Wisconsin, who had been staff director of the Cabinet Committee on Economic Security; and myself, from Princeton University. There were, however, four other public members from outside academia: Henry Bruère, who, while President of the Bowery Savings Bank, had long been active in community welfare programs; Lucy Mason, General Secretary of the National Consumers League, who replaced Josephine Roche, formerly Assistant Secretary of the Treasury; Gerald Morgan, a wise and deeply concerned friend of President Roosevelt; and Elizabeth Wisner, Past President of the Association of Schools of Social Work.

The members of this first Advisory Council have been individually identified because their careful selection and representative stature has proved to be a valuable precedent in the appointment of succeeding Councils. The relative balance between the three groups of employee, employer, and public members has been preserved. The inclusion of a core group of academic economists and others specializing in public policy has continued, as well as the inclusion of leaders from the fields of finance, insurance, medicine, and social work.

The second Advisory Council which served in 1947 and 1948 was established more formally by a Senate resolution and was again responsible to the Senate Finance Committee. Its purpose was to assist the Senate in dealing with legislation "relating to social security hereafter originating in the House of Representatives under the requirements of the Constitution." Its sponsorship by a single branch of Congress did not appear to influence its effectiveness as a link between Congress as a whole and the Social Security Administration. By 1957, however, the value of such general Councils had become sufficiently clear that the Council of 1957-58 was established by formal act of Congress under the Social Security Act amendments of 1956. The Councils of 1963-64 and 1969-71 were likewise established under the provisions of the Act. Under the present legislation, subsequent Councils are to be appointed in 1973 and every four years thereafter. Meanwhile, over the years, the Social Security Administration has been greatly assisted by other advisory groups, usually on specific aspects of the program. The discussion herein has been limited, however, to the activities of the more general Advisory Councils listed above.

Advisory Councils, throughout the years, have had excellent and sustained staff support from the Social Security administration. The chief officers of the administration participate actively in the long series of meetings over the eighteen months or more during which each Council is usually active. Their attendance has been helpful not only in the presentation and discussion of data and in answering questions concerning administrative experience, but also in working out plans for the preparation of scores of studies, drafts, and actuarial analyses. The Treasury and Labor Departments have also assigned experienced representatives to assist the Council. The amount of material prepared for study by Council members can, perhaps, be better visualized by mentioning a bit of practical statistics. The working papers of each member of the most recent Council for study in preparation for its seventeen meetings from June, 1969, to February, 1971, filled twenty-one large loose-leaf binders and, in addition, a full drawer of a correspondence file. As can be seen, much of the work of Councils has been done between the customary two-day sessions in Washington or Baltimore.

The five major Advisory Councils which have served over the thirty-four years since 1937 have built up a body of internal precedents which has greatly enhanced their effectiveness in influencing the philosophy and policy implemented in the American social security system. The author, as chairman of the first Council and as a member of the succeeding four, has been in a good position to watch these precedents evolve and stand the test of time. The special nature of the assignment assumed by each Council in respect to a vast system of social security appears to have predetermined the corporate character and procedures of the body engaged in fulfilling that assignment.

From the first, Councils have come to reflect a sense of *total* responsibility for the integrity and effectiveness of the social security program. While in being for a limited period, the Council assumes, in a very real sense, a function of trusteeship on behalf of the American people in respect to a system in which the vast majority of men, women, and children have an *individual* stake. Councils have been especially directed by Congress to ascertain the financial soundness of each social insurance program.

This sense of total responsibility on the part of the Councils has been enhanced by the need to weigh both the benefit outlays *and* the contribution income over the long future and to assure a proper balancing of these flows as well as the maintenance of adequate reserves. Unlike many advisory bodies, an Advisory Council on Social Security cannot advocate generous benefits in amount or scope and blithefully ignore the costs of those benefits or how those costs should be met. Further, there is the very difficult exercise of responsibility in weighing the specific claims for protection on the part of the old, the survivors, the disabled, and the sick. With a limited flow of funds, hard decisions have to be made. A sense of restraint develops as attractive ideas for the improvement of the benefit structure or coverage must be balanced against each other in terms of actuarially determined costs measured in fractional percentages in the rates of payroll taxes needed to meet those costs.

Another strong precedent, which arises from the sense of responsibility which has developed, is the persistent seeking of consensus. The large measure of influence which the recommendations of the first Advisory Council in 1937-38 had in the revisions of the Social Security Act arose out of their high degree of unanimity. More recent Councils have recognized this, not always with equal success. Despite the tripartite constituency of the

Councils, the long and repeated discussions over many months tend to promote compromise and consensus at least among a larger central core of the membership. There has always been provision for minority statements, however, which have usually reflected some degree of difference in respect to the *rate of change* in the system rather than in its basic principles.

Over the years, Advisory Councils have developed effective procedures in attacking the increasingly complex problems arising in the extension of the social security system. After a general survey of all aspects of the programs covered, both through oral presentation by the staff, and by study of all relevant reports, succeeding meetings are assigned to the consideration of specific problems or improvements. Tentative conclusions or "considerations" are gradually developed, subject always to repeated review in the light of precise costs and countervailing needs for change. As time passes, tentative conclusions which have stood the test are expressed in the specific language of a possible recommendation. The wording of the preliminary recommendation is again tested and retested, with the help of the staff, and is kept in concise form so that full understanding and consensus may be gained on the precise principle expressed. The supporting argument for the evolving recommendation is carefully spelled out and reviewed, but is considered secondary to the recommendation itself, which if finally approved will appear in "bold face" in the Council's report.

By focusing its attention on the hammering out of a series of precisely worded recommendations, which emphasize policy rather than the detailed implementation

51

of policy, Advisory Councils have not invaded the function of either the administration or the legislative staffs of the Congressional committees. Further, in a day when few congressmen can read long reports, a summary listing of precisely worded recommendations will communicate, in short space, the substance of the Council's findings, even if time does not permit study of the full report. The method requires, however, a longer process of study, discussion, and refinement on the part of the Council than most advisory bodies can afford. It requires far more effort in study and discussion to gain a high degree of consensus on a precisely worded recommendation (which may cost a billion dollars to implement) than to gain signatures for pages of noble but indecisive prose.

It is the presence of both the general administrative executives and of the chief planners and actuaries of the Social Security Administration in the sessions of an Advisory Council which makes precision possible in the Council's deliberations. There is constant interchange concerning the relative need, administrative feasibility, interdependence, and estimated cost (in tenths of a percent of payroll tax) of any change. The Council benefits from the views and knowledge of the administration, but the administration also gains from the studied judgments of the members of the Council, long before the final report is completed.

Several other precedents in Council procedure have enhanced the effectiveness of the mechanism. Advisory Councils meet in closed session without publicity. They have avoided the holding of hearings since these are the proper function of the congressional committees when specific legislation is under consideration. Nor do Councils make preliminary reports, since these might foreclose the full and final consideration of an integrated body of recommendations with interlocking costs. For the same reason, no news releases or press interviews are arranged. Every attempt is made to enhance the corporate nature of the Council and the focusing of public attention on its *final* report as a corporate body. When this report is submitted through the Secretary of Health, Education and Welfare for transmission to the Congress and to the Board of Trustees of each of the social security trust funds, the particular Advisory Council ceases to exist.

With their heavy responsibility for examining the financial and actuarial soundness of the social security system, recent Councils have customarily appointed from their membership an actuarial sub-committee of specially qualified persons. This sub-committee has had the continuing help of the actuarial staff of the Social Security Administration. In the most recent Council, a panel of distinguished economists and actuaries outside of government was engaged to assist the sub-committee.

In the ensuing chapters, the reader will come to grips with the issues of philosophy and policy which have concerned repeated Advisory Councils since the Social Security Act was passed in 1935. If the issues are not always easy to resolve, it will be better understood why Advisory Councils have been useful as a link between the administrative and legislative branches of government once our country embarked upon a vast social security system. The outlays of the government under the OASDI and Medicare programs now exceed thirty billion dollars a year, second only to those for defense. It may be unduly biased to remark that the relative degree of assurance on the part of the American people of the wisdom with which these two great outlays are administered is, in some slight degree, influenced by the repeated reviews by external Advisory Councils of the programs herein discussed.

## CHAPTER IV

# Issues Concerning the Function and Scope of OASDI:

# The Proper Relation to Public Assistance

FROM ITS EARLIEST DEVELOPMENT in this country, the purpose of contributory old age insurance has been to build a middle layer of protection for persons in old age which lies between the residual, lower layer of protection provided through relief or assistance on a needs-test basis and an open-end, upper layer of protection acquired by private initiative and by private mechanisms. This three-layer approach has become commonly accepted in principle, but the precise boundaries of the three layers will continue to be subject to debate. In identifying the proper function and scope of contributory social insurance in contrast to other means of protecting persons against adverse contingencies, the relation of social insurance to relief or public assistance will be first discussed. The relation of social insurance benefits to supplementary protection gained through private initiative will then be covered.

Beginning with Montana in 1923, twenty-eight states and two territories had enacted old age assistance programs by January 1, 1935. Such programs were intended to replace the long existing arrangements of caring for the aged poor and others in almshouses or on "poor farms." The conditions for eligibility under these early programs were restrictive, and the standards of payment varied widely. From January 1, 1935, to July, 1935, seven additional states enacted old age assistance laws in anticipation of federal aid under the Social Security Act then under consideration in Congress. It was obvious at that time that federal legislation to assist the states in financing old age assistance, provided certain standards were maintained, would greatly extend the program in both coverage and cost.

An important purpose of the old age insurance provisions of the Social Security Act was to develop a constructive means of controlling the mounting future costs of old age assistance. Estimates then indicated that the aged population of the country would rise from 5.4 percent in 1930 to 12.6 percent in 1990. With the increasing industrialization and urbanization of the country, it was to be expected that a rising proportion of the aged would require assistance, if no other protection were developed. In simple terms, the contributory social insurance mechanism was a means of lifting out an increasing proportion of persons from dependence on old age assistance and thereby controlling a large and mounting outlay by the federal and state governments.

Less tangible, but even more important in terms of morale and motivation in a democratic country, was the fear that a steadily increasing proportion of aged people on needs-test assistance would lead to frustration, bitterness, and resultant political repercussions. The welling emotionalism that supported the Townsend movement was all too evident. An improved system of assistance was obviously needed, but a more constructive program was likewise necessary to limit the assistance approach to its appropriate residual level of protection.

The determination of the proper dividing line between

56

protection by assistance and that by social insurance will always be a matter of judgment. Since determining levels of protection in terms of dollars and minimum household budgets leads to endless debates about surveys and statistics, it is more useful to analyze the issues in principle. No precise boundary can be defined, and overlapping protection to some degree is to be expected. The best approach, therefore, is that of defining the major target zone of each method of protecting persons against the serious contingencies of life.

A simple first approximation in establishing the model area of coverage for public assistance is that it should protect those persons whose earnings under contributory insurance coverage would be inadequate to form a sufficient base for *insured* protection. Social insurance *is* insurance in the sense of relating benefits to a loss of income *normally* received. If the income lost is already inadequate, the benefit would also be inadequate, and reliance on an insurance mechanism would be inappropriate. Only by unreasonably high minimum benefits and unreasonably liberal eligibility standards can the insurance mechanism be distorted to protect adequately persons of low and intermittent earnings. This is the function of assistance.

In practical fact, contributory insurance must establish minimum eligibility and benefit standards which are internally consistent within social insurance policy and with effective use of the administrative machinery of insurance. At some point, the wage earner has contributed sufficiently to assume that he has an earned right to protection. With graduations favorable to persons with relatively low average earnings, the benefits at the minimum will be relatively liberal. The minimum point at which such benefits will be paid cannot be too high since no return of insufficient contributions is made, and the number of contributors who miss out must be relatively small in order to avoid a justifiable sense of grievance. Yet setting the minimum benefit too low leads to extensive overlapping with assistance when it is the major means of protection, and when insurance can do little to help the person. The administrative cost of making small monthly payments over a long period becomes excessively high in terms of social benefit.

On the upper side of the boundary between protection by assistance and that by social insurance, it is a sound working assumption that persons *regularly* employed at even minimum wage levels, as established by law or custom, should receive reasonable insurance protection without resorting to assistance except under exceptional conditions of need. This objective in policy is more readily attainable because of a graduated scale of benefits which provides a larger relative replacement of lost earnings for lower-paid workers. This does not necessarily mean that low earners who are regularly employed receive fully adequate protection in *absolute* terms, but rather that the insurance mechanism can be adjusted in some degree to provide protection at a level which reflects the relative presumptive need of those beneficiaries whose expenditures are heavily concentrated on basic necessities. There is serious question whether a contributory social insurance system can seek to do more without impairing its acceptance by the large body of potential beneficiaries well above the minimum.

The raising of average wages for the lower-paid regularly employed involves economic and legislative factors far beyond the concern of social insurance. There are practical limits to what social insurance can and should do. Beyond reasonable graduations in insurance benefits, the redistribution of national income according to normal levels of earnings should be attained through the instruments of taxation and appropriation including those for public assistance. To use social insurance as a major mechanism to offset low wages is like lifting a dog by its tail. Because social insurance is effective in the limited function for which it is intended does not justify placing burdens upon it which distort its purpose and endanger its acceptance.

If the wage earners of the country were neatly divided between those "regularly" employed under contributory social insurance coverage and those who are not, the boundary between protection by assistance and protection by insurance would be far easier to define. The lifetime pattern of employment for many individuals is, however, affected by business conditions, health, youth, declining physical capacity, obsolescence of skills, marriage and child-rearing, and many other factors. Further, there remain considerable areas of gainful employment in federal and other government employments which appear as voids in the wage record under OASDI. Many potential beneficiaries have low average incomes because they have been unfortunate at some time in life; others because of their decision to remain out of the labor market; and still others because employment under coverage was incidental to or followed long periods of non-covered government employment. In practical terms, a social insurance system cannot avoid overlapping benefits in a considerable proportion of all three types of work patterns. The object of policy should be to limit the overlapping areas to the minimum degree consistent with the internal balance and integrity of the social insurance system and not to permit conditions affecting marginal beneficiaries to justify diversion from the main thrust of the system.

The political pressure to increase social insurance benefits at the lower margin is far greater because of the absence in the United States of a nationwide assistance program with financial support, standards of protection, and administration centered in the federal government. Nature abhors a vacuum and so do the unmet needs of a large segment of the American electorate. No matter how wise the pattern of protection afforded by the OASDI program, it now floats in mid-air above a residual pattern of protection by assistance which is fragmented and distorted by a multitude of political, economic, and cultural factors.

To form a firm upward boundary for the assistance system of the United States does not require that there be a flat, nationwide floor in terms of dollars per person aided. It requires, rather, a consistent meeting of need on the basis of a consistent pattern of determining need. A system of assistance, as a residual means of protection, must be flexible in meeting need as determined in the individual case. There can be, however, national minimum standards of assistance below which no person or family without other means can be expected to exist. With an adequate, yet flexible, national system of assistance related to the residual need of those who for various reasons have no adequate earnings base for social insurance, the lower boundary of social insurance protection could be more firmly established.

Social insurance and public assistance are distinctly different mechanisms for the protection of people against untoward contingencies. Both have internal requirements for effective performance. Like the two wheels of a cart, they can effectively support a load if they are reasonably matched in size and strength. If they are not so matched, the cart lunges to the weak side and the stronger wheel cannot save the cart from disaster. The difficulty of determining the lower limit of social insurance protection is not, in the main, a problem of social insurance policy. It is rather a long unrecognized problem in the financing and administration of public assistance in a nation in which social standards and human resources can no longer be left to sporadic local concern.

The firm foundation of an adequate, national system of public assistance would permit the OASDI system of contributory social insurance to perform more effectively in its own area of protection. Relieved of the pressure to raise the level of minimum benefits beyond that reflecting rising costs of living, the insurance system could further improve the pattern of differential benefits above the minimum. With higher ceilings in the coverage of earnings, there is need to assure reasonable treatment of persons of higher average earnings. The "bend-points" at which the ratios of benefit to rising segments of average earnings change could be further refined to adjust to changing living costs and the presumptive pattern of need. Rising rates of contribution to the OASDI system

61

and its increasing maturity as the normal span of coverage lengthens will require the constant study of the benefit scale in both total level and internal graduations.

Just as contributory social insurance was intended, from the beginning, to lift persons out of the need for old age assistance, so it has come to lift out other categories from needs-test relief. Surviving widows and children were the first to be added to those protected. Later the disabled were covered. The introduction of Medicare relieved millions of the need to resort to assistance when cash benefits were insufficient for health costs in old age. An extension of Medicare to the disabled is a logical next step. In each case, an insurable risk has been defined, and the insurance mechanism has been used to lift persons out of reliance on the residual relief system by providing protection as a matter of right.

But even in a prosperous country there will always be large segments of the population for whom public assistance will be a necessary protection against insecurity and hardship. Social insurance seeks to extend normal self-sufficiency into periods when some contingency such as old age, disability, ill-health, or death *interrupts* self-sufficiency of the person or his family. Where there is no reasonable basis because of gainful employment to establish eligibility and benefits related to contribution, the insurance mechanism becomes ineffective. The major area for public assistance is therefore the protection of those who for protracted periods in life are unable to support themselves or their families adequately. The secondary area for public assistance is to fill in the chinks and margins of a social security system where (a) the government has failed to recognize a category of insurable risks or to meet them adequately on the basis of presumptive need through social insurance, or (b) the conditions of need in the *individual* case require exceptional protection beyond the predetermined benefits provided by insurance. As an integrated, wage-related system, social insurance must operate within specific definitions, benefit scales, and limits. In this respect it lacks the flexibility of an assistance program. An assistance program, being residual, must retain its flexibility to close in the gaps of need both by uncovered categories and in the individual case.

The question has been raised whether a nationally administered, nationally financed public assistance program might not some day raise its standards of protection to the point where the middle zone of social insurance would lose its appeal for many. There are several reasons for believing that such a situation is unlikely to occur. The assumption that contributory social insurance pays benefits to the participant as a matter of right is deeply embedded in American psychology. Public assistance, by whatever name, is still needs-test relief based on an individual's condition determined at the time of payment. No streamlining of qualification procedures will dissipate the belief that assistance is intended to mitigate a lack of self-sufficiency after the fact. Further, assistance is related to specific deficits against a minimal norm, whereas social insurance provides rising differentials related to past contributions. Finally, the benefits under social insurance are so much a matter of right in the minds of the participant and his employer that they have become coordinated with the industrial benefit programs of the country. Public assistance, by its very character, can never be so coordinated. The payment of a minimally adequate retirement annuity or insurance benefit would automatically eliminate eligibility for assistance.

In practical terms, the likelihood that a national system of public assistance would seriously encroach upon the role of social insurance is slight because of the great cost of raising the standards of assistance payments sufficiently to make possible favorable comparison with insurance. To be "competitive," public assistance would need not only to establish a modest floor of payments, but also make differential payments related to the cost of living in various parts of the country. Further, such payments would need to be made at the same time to great categories not covered by insurance. Without the highly effective mechanism of the payroll tax, the cost of such payments would become a heavy burden on the general budget. It is unlikely that public support could be gained for the taxes required to finance them.

The general conclusion seems justified that an effective national system of public assistance is greatly needed to undergird an effective national system of contributory social insurance. Each system has its own role to play. Some overlapping at the boundaries of protection in individual cases is inevitable, but the appropriate zones of service can and should remain clear. The greatest danger is that the absence of an effective national system of public assistance will lead to pressures for raising the minimum benefits under insurance in a way which will distort that insurance mechanism's proper role of *preventing* dependency and reduce its acceptance as a contributory mechanism providing benefits related to previous contribution.

## CHAPTER V

# Issues Concerning the Function and Scope

# of OASDI:

# The Proper Relation to Private Mechanisms

# for Protection

O NE OF THE TOUGHEST battles in the legislative development of the Social Security Act in 1935 was over the issue whether the new federal old age insurance program should parallel rather than undergird industrial pension plans. Through the proposed Clark Amendment, an effort was made by certain representatives of the insurance industry to include in the Act a provision whereby approved company group annuity plans could substitute for compulsory coverage under old age insurance.

The supporters of an effective social insurance program vigorously opposed the Clark Amendment for several reasons. Most pressing was the fear that such an amendment, by requiring specific interlocking provisions between the contributions required under the taxing power and benefits paid under the appropriations power of the federal government, would endanger the constitutionality of the Act. It was also believed that contracting out of coverage would lead to grave administrative difficulties for both the government and the companies involved, and might well impair the certainty of protection on a nationwide basis of workers as they moved from employer to employer throughout life.

A more fundamental objection to the Clark Amendment for contracting out of coverage was that it undermined the basic concept that a national old age insurance system should form a solid, consistent, and integrated layer of protection undergirding *all* private mechanisms for the prevention of dependency in old age. Responsible for its citizens and otherwise obligated to help meet the costs of relief or assistance, the national government sought a universal form of protection which would lift its citizens out of fear of dependency and, at the same time, reward incentive. According to this concept, the government was establishing a privilege of American citizenship which was deeper and broader than the privilege of working for any private employer, no matter how enlightened.

It is fortunate that a number of larger, more progressive companies saw that their interest in a common floor of contributory protection coincided with that of the government. They also came to see that contracting out would involve bothersome and perhaps costly regulation of private programs to assure that, in standards and financing, they afforded protection equal to that of the government program. Even stable employers recognized that many workers would not continue in their employ throughout their working lives and that a sticky problem of vesting company contributions as workers shifted from company coverage to social insurance coverage would arise. It was decided by those company executives who took the time to study the problem that it would be preferable to avoid entanglements and to revise their retirement annuity programs to form a private, supplementary form of protection which built upon a national base of old age insurance.

The removal of the threat of contracting out under the Clark Amendment was a greater contribution to a sound old age insurance system than many realized at the time. With the elimination of the possibility of parallel alternative coverage, the advantages of a three-level system of assistance, social insurance, and private mechanisms, as visualized by the planners of old age insurance, gained increasing acceptance. With clarification of the issue of substitution of *forms*, that of proper determination of the appropriate *levels* of protection became the continuing issue. While company group annuity programs are but one kind of supplementary protection, they are, because of their size of coverage, organization, contractual nature, actuarial complexity, and financial costs, the private protective mechanism which is most affected by the precise upper limits of social insurance coverage.

To understand the sensitivity of private pension programs to varying levels of social insurance coverage, it is necessary to analyze the function of company retirement annuity programs. Although started years ago as a means of providing relief for superannuated employees, in the last half-century they have become an important device of personnel administration for displacing older workers and yet maintaining the effectiveness of an ongoing organization. To displace workers at a set retirement age without loss of morale on the part of those continuing in employment, a company retirement plan can no longer pay benefits related to personal need alone, but must, in its scale, bear close relation to the past service and compensation of the employee. In effect, a company retirement annuity has become an extension of the contract of employment with differentials fully reflecting the

67

past economic contribution of the individual. Since the principle of contract has replaced that of imputed need, graduations in benefits favorable to low-income employees are out of place. In superimposing a private annuity program upon a universal social insurance program, therefore, the employer is faced with the problem of coordinating two benefit structures: one, social insurance, in which benefits are graduated in some degree according to imputed need, and the other, a company annuity program, in which differentials must closely reflect past earnings and service in the company. The latter differentials must extend far higher than the ceiling for coverage and benefits under social insurance.

So long as the ceiling of covered wages under the uniform social insurance tax rate is at a moderate level, adjustments in a company annuity plan on both the contribution and benefit sides can assure a relatively reasonable compromise between the two principles in benefit structure. A *drastic* rise in the social insurance tax ceiling, however, forces the employer to meet a much higher tax cost for higher-income employees who are near or above the new ceiling without a comparable sharing of the cost of the higher-level benefits which he must provide under his own annuity program. An increased segment of his tax cost will have been used to assure favorable benefits for lower-income workers in general under the social insurance program, but he must still meet the supplementary cost of preserving full differentials for his own higher-income employees under his company retirement program. There are limits to the extent to which the employer can shift this supplementary cost to his higher-salaried employees, since their contributions to the social insurance program would also have risen drastically.

The need to adjust the two systems of insurance protection of older employees will continue. Both principles of benefit structure are sound. The solution lies in a reasonable determination from time to time of the segment of worker earnings which should be the base for a uniform payroll tax for a socially graduated benefit and of the remainder which should be the base for supplementary, privately determined protection. Social insurance benefits do reflect incentive in considerable degree, but they are graduated according to imputed need. There is still a great need in a dynamic economy for protective programs which reflect individual incentive more fully and directly and which supplement social insurance beyond its zone of concern. The employer, facing the need to sustain incentive at first hand, has a justifiable stake in assuring the effectiveness of his total compensation structure, including retirement annuities, in this perennial effort.

Since the combination of a directly proportionate tax and a graduated benefit results in a net gain to a social insurance system when the ceiling of covered wages is raised, there is need for restraint in pushing up the ceiling, once reasonably established, faster than is justified by the rise in the overall patterns of earnings in the country. While there is nothing sacred in the precise segment of real earnings which OASDI has covered over the past twenty years, it is seen to have been reasonably consistent when the timing of adjustments is averaged out. A continuance of the same proportionate segment of overall real earnings seems justified by the practical test of long acceptance. This will require that increases in the ceiling will parallel the increases in overall earnings, so that the proper zone of protection by social insurance will be maintained. There is no more argument to *narrow* this zone of protection under social insurance as earnings rise than to *invade* the zone of private means of protection beyond the proportionate segment in real terms now established.

In order to justify a drastic rise in the ceiling of tax coverage under OASDI, some proponents have claimed that the ceiling should carry forward the proportionate coverage of overall average earnings reflected in the $3,000 ceiling in the Social Security Act of 1935. As a participant in the setting of that ceiling, the author can testify that it was based on a very limited evidence at a time when few, if any, guidelines existed. The rates of contribution and the whole benefit structure have been drastically altered since then. The last twenty years, during which OASDI has established its role as a part of a three-level program of protection against life contingencies in this country, are far more relevant in determining its proper zone of coverage than a ceiling set *a priori* by the planners of an untried program.

The issue remains whether the ceiling on covered earnings under OASDI should be adjusted automatically by a formula permanently established in the legislation or from time to time by specific congressional action. The need for a smooth and orderly adjustment of the ceiling to the overall pattern of earnings in the country is difficult to deny. Even more evident is the need for orderly and sensitive adjustment of benefit scales to a rising cost of living. Since the two forms of adjustment are closely interrelated, they can be considered jointly.

Would the automatic adjustment of the ceiling of covered earnings or an automatic adjustment of benefit scales to cost of living, tend unduly to freeze the existing *pattern* of benefits in the program? The OASDI benefit structure involves more than minimums, maximums, and general levels. The slope of graduations relating benefits to an individual's average covered wages needs constant review. The balance of benefits among various categories of beneficiaries, such as between married couples and widows, may require readjustment. Whole new categories of beneficiaries will require consideration. If the benefits now established for some may need to be held back in order to improve the benefits of others, would not a rigid, automatic formula create assumed rights which will harden resistance to reopening the benefit structure? It would be the higher-income workers, whose taxes are most affected by a higher ceiling, who would be most sensitive to a loss of expected gains in benefit amount if a rigid formula, once established, was not observed.

If firm expectancies were to be created by a rigid, automatic formula for ceilings and benefit levels, it would be necessary to premise that the income of the system would be sufficient in the years ahead to make needed improvements in the overall pattern of benefits as well as to meet the automatic increases in currently established schedules. An increase in tax ceilings cannot be assumed to meet the increased benefit rights arising directly from the new ceilings, a general automatic increase in benefit *scale*, reflecting cost of living, *and also* any improvements

71

in overall benefit *pattern* which may prove desirable. A need to change the slope of the benefit scale from time to time would add further costs. Nor can contribution rates be raised indefinitely. In sum, it must be concluded that the introduction of a rigidly enforced automaticity in a part of a social insurance mechanism, no matter how desirable, in itself reduces the degree of flexibility which remains in planning the total system in the years ahead.

On balance, it appears that a creative compromise is possible in gaining the advantages of automatic adjustment in contribution ceilings and the level of benefits and, at the same time, avoiding a premature freezing of benefit structure and coverage. This is to provide that automatic adjustments take place *only* if Congress has *not* acted in revising the program either in or effective in the year previous to that in which an automatic adjustment would otherwise take place under the established formula. Such an arrangement would permit Congress to retain the initiative in a continuing evolution of the system. At the same time, it would provide a greater sense of security on the part of current beneficiaries and all potential beneficiaries that the level of benefits, and an important means of financing them, would not suffer attrition if the value of the dollar declined, even though Congress were too busy to act on compensating adjustments.

The position taken in respect to the need to leave an upper zone of the earnings base free of social insurance contribution, and therefore available for the financing of private pension plans, assumes that the effectiveness of private pension plans will continue to improve as a means of protection of those coming under them. More immediately justified as an instrument of corporate or institutional personnel policy and, therefore, traditionally in the area of private initiative, private pension plans have increasingly become the object of public interest and concern. Only if the employers of the country recognize this fact, will the people as a whole abide by the long-established premise that the OASDI system should avoid encroaching upon an area reserved for private supplementary programs.

The elements of public interest in private pension plans are several. First is the obvious fact that such plans have accumulated large financial reserves which are, essentially, held in trust for millions of future beneficiaries. The investment or other use of such funds are of concern to the government not only because the interest of millions of citizens is involved, but also for the reason that their assignment to pension reserves as a current cost of doing business is a factor in tax liability. Further, the vast size of private pension reserves has come to make them a significant factor in the capital markets of the country. The reckless administration or arbitrary investment of such large amounts of capital may distort the economy or cause critical instabilities. Funds virtually held in trust for employees on their retirement may, through unwise use, adversely affect their economic security in their working years. The great financial power implicit in large and growing pension reserves is bound to arouse public concern.

The broadening interest in private pension plans is evidenced, also, by the increasing degree to which such plans have become the focus of trade union collective bargaining. No longer are private pension plans in many industries an *ex parte* creation of the employer. They have become a precise element in a collectively negotiated contract between a national union and an employer, whether corporate, institutional, or governmental. While the features of the agreed-upon program are the result of collective bargaining by employer and union representatives, the vital and continuing stake in the plan is that of individuals for the remainder of their lives. The individual, therefore, must be protected from arbitrary or irresponsible action, even on the part of his own agents. The security of the individual and his family, not the immediate interest, political power, or personal aggrandizement of the negotiators of pension agreements, is the social justification of private pension plans. This is true whether a plan is financed and operated by the employer, the union, or jointly. The examples of maladministration under all three arrangements have accentuated public concern.

While the public interest in the financial integrity and equitable administration of private pension plans will continue to mount as they become a larger factor in our economy, the development of OASDI and the growth of general concern for lifelong security has brought into focus a serious shortcoming in most private pension plans as a third level of a three-tier system of social security. This is the lack of adequate provisions for vesting in a large proportion of such plans. Under OASDI, the earnings of the individual employee continue to his credit in the eventual determination of his benefit, regardless of shifts in employment throughout life. The OASDI program thus embodies in its operation the principle of immediate and permanent vesting in the individual of all credits to his account. With few exceptions, such as under the plan of the Teachers' Insurance and Annuity Association program covering universities and colleges, private pension programs vest credits to the permanent account of the employee only at certain attained ages or after varying periods of service, from a few years to that of a normal working life.

The effect of delayed vesting under private pension plans is to reduce greatly their effectiveness as a supplementary layer in a national pattern of social security. The proportion of American wage earners or salaried employees who continue in the employment of a single firm for the forty years from age 25 to age 65 may be increasing, but the fraction is still far lower than even the best of employers assume. The causes of interrupted service are compounded by conditions affecting the employer, such as business conditions, technological and product change, mergers, shifts in location, and administrative policy. On the part of the employee, interruptions are caused by shifting factors of health, interest, rate of compensation, growth in capacity, living and transportation arrangements, and personal compatibility. One cannot expect this complex of factors to change in the absence of a regimented state. Therefore, the adverse effects of interrupted and shifting employment throughout working life upon the protection afforded must be greatly attenuated if private pension plans are to fulfill their proper role as an important segment in the social security system of the country.

The response of the American employer to this argument is that a mechanism of private enterprise is not intended to solve social problems. It harks back to a simpler

75

assumption of the function of private pension plans as an employer-initiated method of displacing superannuated employees without general loss of morale, or of attracting and holding employees in the competitive market for qualified personnel. But the economics of employee compensation has shifted drastically since the time when fringe benefits, including pension plans, were the mark of the exceptional employer. The fringe has now become a part of the cloth. A contract of employment today, whether signed or assumed, increasingly embodies or involves a range of financial arrangements extending beyond immediate cash compensation. It has become apparent that the eventual protection of the employee in his old age is now too significant a part of the contract of employment to be left to the fortuitous circumstance of long years of continued employment with a single employer. This is clear in the attitudes of labor leaders. It will become increasingly clear in the attitudes of employees, especially those in greatest demand.

It would be easy to suggest the logical corrective that pension credits in private employment should be vested immediately in the employee in parallel with cash compensation. In this way, the concurrent and future return to the employee for work performed and the full cost to the employer in both cash and pension contributions for that work would be contemporaneous, pay period by pay period. This would assure a neat and conservative method of cost accounting, as well as contributing to the eventual security of the employee. But given the method of financing almost all private pension plans today, it would be very expensive. It is the usual practice to reduce the amount of funding of such plans to take account of actual or expected turnover between the time of employment or eligibility and the time of complete vesting. Even if costs were not so great, employers would object to assigning and funding pension credits to some categories of employees.

The problem of vesting under private pension plans has a long history. It was, as noted earlier, one of the reasons why leading corporations soon lost interest in the Clark Amendment advanced by certain insurance carriers in 1935. Under this proposal to permit contracting out from coverage under the Social Security Act, private employers would have faced the strong probability that contributions equivalent to those required under old age insurance would need to be transmitted to the government whenever an employee left an employer who had contracted out of coverage. This would have involved, in effect, an approach to partial, immediate vesting, since concurrent credits and funding in respect to each employee would have become the only effective method of meeting government standards for contracting out from social security coverage.

Instead of becoming tied into a general social insurance program in this way, leading employers in 1935 decided to keep their pension programs as distinct in plan, financing, and administration as possible. For many years, this decision appeared reasonable. But the degree of distinction desired is no longer as easy to maintain as it was when old age insurance contributions and benefits were relatively small. Despite many other adjustments required by both social insurance and tax legislation, however, the sharp contrast between immediate vesting under OASDI and long-delayed vesting under most pri-

77

vate pension plans has retained a high order of visibility. It now appears that the employers' decision in 1935 to avoid entanglement *in fact* did not eliminate a persistent social pressure over the years for compatibility *in principle*, once the social security program had gained maturity and full public acceptance. The failure of private pension programs to move more rapidly to the principle of immediate vesting has become a serious shortcoming in our national pattern of protecting our older citizens.

With the great costs involved in shifting to the provision of immediate vesting in private pension programs and the need to recognize that such plans remain an instrument of effective personnel administration, it may be well to suggest a workable compromise as a goal in a gradual shift in corporate pension policy. This goal might be that, within a period of time, pension credits accruing under private programs would become permanently vested in the employee after the completion of not more than two years of service with an employer for persons over a certain age, perhaps twenty-nine, and after the completion of not more than five years of service for younger persons. This would relieve the employer of the cost of funding pension credits for young people, whose turnover is usually high, or for short-time employees of any age. For the very young, the effect of the loss of early credits would be minimal. For many older, short-time employees, it is probable that OASDI will be their major source of protection in any case. Such a goal, if attained, would go far to make private pension programs a compatible and effective instrument of old age security supplementary to OASDI. It would also go far to sustain the justification of a three-level pattern of social security in a country in which the pension policies of larger corporations, institutions, and governmental agencies so greatly affect the adequacy and equitable coverage of a three-level program. From the point of view of the country's employers, it would greatly strengthen their position that the contribution ceilings under OASDI should not be raised to a level which curtails their ability to provide adequately for their higher-income employees in a manner which enhances incentive and rewards, more fully and directly than does OASDI, their differential contribution to the firm.

Thus far, the discussion here of the proper relation of social insurance to private mechanisms for protection has centered upon the interrelation of OASDI with private company annuity programs and upon the ceiling on covered earnings, because these are the two areas in which the upper limit of social insurance protection becomes both strategic and apparent in terms of national policy. There are, however, broader and less obvious considerations in fitting a social insurance program into a three-layer system of public assistance, social insurance, and private measures for personal security.

No matter how extensive and adequate a system of social insurance becomes, there are definite limits to the degree to which it can meet the widely diverse needs for protection of a normally self-sufficient family. In the United States today, the hazards of loss of job or of heavy medical costs during working life must still be met in large part through personal savings. One of the most effective means of protection is ownership of a home. The maintenance of customary standards of living by all those above a bare minimum, when contingencies occur, is possible only by the accumulation of private resources through individual initiative.

It is an obligation in social insurance planning in a country such as the United States to weigh seriously how much of a regularly employed worker's income should be channeled into specifically defined areas of protection and how much should be left for him to conserve as a general cushion against unexpected needs. Social insurance has great advantages both in spreading risks and in enforcing foresight. By imposing upon the individual the priorities based on the imputed needs of all, it may, if carried too far, reduce unduly the flexibility of the individual in planning for his individual needs. In earlier times, a farmer improved his farm as a protection in old age when his son would take over. A craftsman or shopkeeper invested in his business. An age-old method of family protection was the education of sons. Social insurance, in an industrial era, requires a degree of conformance to a standard pattern. The question will always remain to what degree conformance should be required in the building of family protection and how large a segment of income should remain available for individual measures for security.

CHAPTER VI

# Issues Related to Contributions by Workers and Employers

## CONTRIBUTIONS BY WORKERS

COMPARED to poor relief or public assistance, social insurance is a very specialized social instrument. To understand its special character, it is necessary to understand its long evolution from the various types of mutual aid societies whereby workers joined together to protect themselves against the hazards of life and industrial employment. Whereas poor relief and assistance grew out of the compassion sanctioned by religion or the policy of governments in avoiding the untoward repercussions of indifference to the needs of the poor, social insurance had its roots in the desire of gainfully employed workers to protect themselves. Social insurance, therefore, traditionally involves a form of social organization for mutual protection similar to the state itself. It differs from the state in that the special protection sought is not against external aggression or internal violence, but against distress caused by loss of income normally available for self-support. Further, the form of organization was normally developed by groups in society who were dependent upon current income from work rather than upon the returns from the ownership of economic assets.

It is still important in the development of social insurance policy to keep in mind this long evolution of the concept. Social institutions which survive over time must in some way respond to the aspirations and common judgment of people. They are not likely to be the sudden inventions of clever planners. Social insurance should be regarded conceptually as a cooperative institution taken over by the state, but still a reflection of the responses of workers who are willing to contribute from their earnings today to protect themselves and their families from the hazards of tomorrow.

A basic strength of the OASDI program in the United States is that it *has* carried forward this concept of mutual self-help out of which social insurance evolved. Unemployment insurance in America, in contrast, was from the beginning strongly influenced by a concept of controlling the incidence of unemployment by varying the charges upon the employer. The latter approach was a carry-over from workmen's compensation insurance, which was more an effort to rationalize the vagaries of litigation under employers' liability laws than a true form of evolving social insurance. With so much emphasis in unemployment insurance upon controlling the incidence of unemployment through differential contributions by the *employer*, the role of the *employee* in helping to protect himself was minimized almost to the vanishing point. More stable employers were so anxious to obtain preferential rates of contribution that they had little interest in demanding joint contributions by their employees. State governments competed in permitting favorable "merit" ratings which lowered the costs of industries they sought to hold or attract. Workers, on their part, finding many employers more concerned about differential contributions than about the adequate protection of the unemployed, regardless of the cause of their unemployment, saw little reason for joining in the financing of the system.

82

In this way, a valuable tradition in social insurance was crowded out by an exaggerated emphasis upon the possibility of controlling the risk for which insurance was provided.

Fortunately, the risks against which OASDI were developed were not assumed to be so directly susceptible to employer influence. Men and women grow old, die, and leave survivors as the universal risks of life. The appeal of mutual self-help, traditional in social insurance, gained ready response. No objection was raised by the representatives of labor to an equal sharing of cost. The author clearly remembers a conversation with William Green, then President of the American Federation of Labor, in November 1934, in which Mr. Green stated bluntly that the American labor movement would go along with "fifty-fifty" contributions to old age insurance "because everyone gets old." But, he added, workers "should not pay a cent" for unemployment insurance since it was the employer who laid men off. Mr. Green, despite years of widespread unemployment, was willing to place the major blame for the condition of the country upon the employers, if they wished to accept it, rather than upon fundamental and dynamic forces within the economy.

It is interesting to speculate why workers continued to be willing to contribute to social insurance after the state took over the function of mutual benefit societies. The reasons appear to be deep in attitudes and common judgments of people which are more persistent than sophisticated theories in politics or economics. There is something of the concept of social contract, first, among participants and, second, between the participants and the government as representing society, that by contributing a person gains a right to a benefit as distinct from any discretionary largesse granted by the state. It is an age-old assumption in folk wisdom that "in this world, you don't get something for nothing." In accepting relief, it is sensed, one gives up a cherished attribute of self-reliance. In receiving an insurance benefit, no matter how complex the financial and actuarial arrangements may be, one is involved in the fulfillment of a contract between responsible parties under which an investment assures a return.

Economists who attempt to dissect out the elements of a contributory social insurance program in terms of taxes and the redistribution of funds often lose sight of this vital principle of mutual contract which runs through the program as a whole. Like any living organism, a social insurance system is more than the sum of its parts. For the economic analyst, the mystique of common habits of mind appears tenuous indeed, yet it is this mystique which has assured the survival and growth of a valuable social mechanism.

In political terms, the contributor to social insurance senses that his direct and defined financial support of the system helps to preserve the assumption that the system is something distinct, as a social mechanism, from the general financial apparatus of government. In most appropriations by government, the Congress or other legislative body grants or withholds funds on the basis of public policy or practical politics. With social security payments, there is, also, an underlying sense of obligation to fulfill an assumed contract with the contributors to the system. The existence of this sense of obligation,

84

while seldom noted by economic analysts, is, again, a part of the mystique of the acceptance by workers of the contributory feature in social insurance.

More understandable to the general taxpayer is another by-product of the social-contract attribute of contributory social insurance. This is the assumption that workers will be more responsible in their demands for higher benefits or extended coverage under a social insurance system if they are paying a predetermined share of the cost. There is justification for this assumption. Responsibility in a contract works both ways. It does not mean, however, that workers, as a group, must forever provide a particular share of the cost of the system. Such rigidity is hard to maintain when some workers are self-employed and some are young and face a long period of contribution. It might justify an employee contribution of one-half the cost, as in OASDI today, or of one-third the cost, as in some other systems.

The foregoing summary of the evolution of the feature of worker contributions in social insurance is the preamble for a much-needed refutation of the arguments of well-intentioned liberals and economic analysts who would alter the concept of a uniform employee contribution in social insurance out of the context of its long-tested acceptance. To them, an employee contribution is a tax like other taxes. Since it is a uniform tax on all earnings below a fixed ceiling, it is, as a "tax," regressive in its total effect. (In dissecting the system into its parts, the fact that benefits are graduated in favor of the lower-income participant is set aside.) Since it is assumed that all regressive taxes are bad, the uniform tax under social insurance is bad and should be changed.

If a social insurance contribution were merely an income tax payment for the support of the general purposes of government, there would be justification of the criticism that, as a tax, it is regressive in effect. Perhaps the large flow of collections which has developed has led to a confusion with the personal income tax. But a social insurance contribution is, first, a part of an integrated social mechanism. Second, it is a tax or contribution dedicated to a specific purpose and related to specific benefits accruing to the contributor. The concept of a progressive rate schedule in income taxes for the general support of the state is a relatively recent and socially justified invention in public policy. To carry it over into the determination of social insurance contributions, as if they were just a special form of income tax, is to proceed on the basis of an *a priori* abstraction which ignores all but the narrow approach of one segment of economics, public finance, in dealing with a long-evolving social institution. The intent to help the poor is commendable. The effect might well be the impairment of a mechanism which has done more to prevent poverty than any other program of government.

To suggest the nature of a social insurance contribution as a dedicated tax for a special purpose in which the contributor benefits, it may help to compare it with other dedicated taxes of less spectacular effect. The question may be posed in each case whether the tax should be levied at progressive rates according to the total earnings of the taxpayer rather than on the basis of the benefit gained. The list could include drivers' licenses, automobile taxes, highway taxes on trucks according to weight, tolls on throughways and bridges, hunting and fishing

86

licenses, and assessments on street improvements. Running through all these forms of charges is the understanding that the private taxpayer is getting something specific for his money. He is not contributing merely to the general costs of government nor is he aggrieved that the charge is not adjusted to his individual, personal income. In the examples given, there is seldom *more* benefit for *less* contribution as in social insurance to lessen further the likelihood of objection to the scale of charges for the benefit received.

Contributory social insurance, as an integrated system, has the aim of preventing reliance upon needs-test assistance on the part of the participant. To introduce an exemption from contribution because of the presumed need of persons of low earnings is to bring back into the system a conceptual approach which is inconsistent with its purpose and with the assumptions of the participants in its long evolution. Again, those who propose the elimination of social insurance contributions by lower-income workers fail to understand the attitudes of the participants. As economic analysts abstracting out the feature of "taxes," or as persons whose humane sympathies are more evident than their understanding of social insurance, they would deprive the "poor" of a sense of self-reliance which they have come to cherish. It is an important consideration in any step to alter the proportional contribution to OASDI that there has never been any pressure from the lower segment of contributors to change the proportionate method of determining the rate of contributions.

A graduated scale of rebates of contributions, declining as earnings rise, lessens only in degree the objections against a total elimination of contributions by lower-income workers. Further, so long as a social insurance system depends for its financing upon the contributions from workers and employers alone, a decrease in income from the lower-paid would need to be offset by a progressive scale of contributions by the higher-paid worker and his employer. Since the higher-income participant receives a lower relative benefit, any strain on the acceptance of the contributory system, as rates of contribution rise, would be increased. Rather than endanger this acceptance, which involves so intimately the concept of mutual benefit, it is far more reasonable to introduce the concept of progressive taxation through a government contribution to the social insurance system, drawing upon the general tax sources of the government. The great advantage of using progressive income taxes for such a government contribution is that tax levies would not be limited to any segment of covered earnings from employment or to any particular kind of income. Further, such progressive income taxes, merged with the general program of government support, would avoid any confusion with a social insurance program of mutual protection providing specific benefits.

Any departure from a directly proportional rate of contribution by workers under contributory social insurance involves many other problems. The precise matching of employer and employee contributions under OASDI has been accepted in the United States for a third of a century. Again a concept of mutuality of responsibility has become established. Should the employer alone finance the benefits of lower-income employees; should the employer and his higher-paid employees make up for the contributions forgiven; or should the government replace the contributions lost? If the government is asked to make up the loss, there are far better ways to use the large subsidy required for the elimination or reduction of contributions by lower-income workers.

Apart from objections in principle, there are problems of policy and procedure in rebating the contributions of lower-income workers. Should only *covered* earnings be the basis for determining a rebate, or all earnings, or all income regardless of kind or source? Should the "need" of the contributor in terms of size of family be considered or, on the other hand, the earnings of the family unit? Further, there is the problem of multiple employers, either concurrent or over time, during an earnings period. If each employer reduced the payroll deduction made for OASDI against a first segment of earnings, either a great loss to the system would result or many would need to reimburse the system later. Only by a periodic report of both income and exemptions, such as under the income tax collections, could a proper determination of the rebate be made. This would greatly complicate the operation of the internal revenue service at a level where simplification has long been sought. It would also involve the lower-income worker in claims procedures and long delays in recovering a contribution which he now assumes to be a reasonable charge for a specific, individual benefit.

## Contributions by Employers

The participation of employers in the support of a social insurance system is generally taken for granted. The concept that an employer is responsible for the welfare of those working for him, whether slave or free, existed in the earliest stages of civilization. It appears in Roman law and feudal customs. Only in that period of rapid technological change called the Industrial Revolution did the concept become submerged for a time by a conscience-less and shortsighted misapplication of the principles of laissez-faire economics. It was then that economics earned the title of the "dismal science." It was an early manifestation of the danger of applying abstract economic analysis, unalloyed by a study of human institutions, to the development of public policy.

Fortunately, the concept of employer responsibility has re-emerged in the present century, at first stimulated by legislation and trade union pressure, and later by the growing social conscience and enlightened self-interest of progressive employers. It is interesting to note that in respect to employee protection related to death and old age, progressive American corporations began developing programs a half-century ago, at a time when governments and the trade unions were still concentrating their efforts on wages, hours, and working conditions.

The acceptance by the larger American corporation of the obligation to pay contributions to a social insurance program, although influenced by the traditional concept of employer responsibility, was probably more directly the result of the need for a perpetual corporation to assure a flow of effective and well-motivated personnel for the year-by-year operation of the company. Retirement programs with adequate pensions became necessary to prevent an excessive aging of staff or the loss of morale which the discard of the old without compensation would involve. Such programs became a charge on current production to be passed on to the consumer. Group life insurance proved a valuable fringe benefit in making employment with a company more attractive both in recruitment and in reducing turnover.

By 1934, at the time the OASDI program was being developed, a number of leading companies in the United States had become convinced that "fringe benefits" were an essential element in a sound personnel program and that their costs could be considered, in part, at least, as a charge upon the cost of production. The assignment of such costs to a cost per employee, related to wages paid, was a logical step in both current budgeting and in actuarial evaluation of future costs. Where contributions were asked of the employee, the principle of a sharing of costs, year by year, with each employee became accepted.

It was fortunate that the employer representatives who were active in the early planning of the old age insurance part of the Social Security Act had gone through a period of development of fringe benefits in their own corporations. The transfer of a concept of sound practice in their own corporation to sound practice in what was to be a nationwide personnel program for the protection of superannuated workers, generally, appeared reasonable. A sharing of costs related to earnings, year by year, to assure rights to benefit, was justified as an appropriate division of costs assigned to production and costs assigned to individual potential beneficiary. The employer gained in meeting costs already assumed, and the employee gained in a more universal form of protection.

The transfer of the principle of sharing the costs of old age protection from a private to a social insurance

91

context was made easier for the larger, progressive corporation because the cost had already been assumed by them but *not* by some of their less progressive competitors. The perpetual corporation recognized that it faced the problem of superannuation and obsolescence in manning its operations. The smaller or less enlightened employer, in most cases, was still avoiding the added costs of production which adequate retirement programs involved. It was in the interest of the larger, perpetual corporation that this element of costs be made uniform, at least on a minimal basis.

The more specific reasons for the support of employer contributions in the evolution of old age insurance in the United States explains to some degree why an equal division of costs seemed reasonable to corporate executives. The contribution to be charged employers under the public program was a partial replacement *for particular individuals* of a segment of a cost already borne. The measure of the employer's contribution to the social insurance system should be, it was assumed, the amount the employee contributed, no more, no less. The employer's contribution was not a general tax payment related to the whole of an employee's salary or to the profits of the corporation. The financing of the social insurance program, again, reflected the concept of a mutual contract, in this respect, between the employer and employee in the terms of employment, even though required by the state. In such a mutual contract, a "fifty-fifty" sharing of cost was supported by an "aesthetic logic" which no other ratio exhibited.

The line of thought which led employers to accept equal contributions for old age insurance would also lead

92

them to object strenuously to a proposal, sometimes advanced, that the employer contribution to social insurance should not be limited to the same segment of earnings on which the employee contributes. Apart from the heavy costs involved, the employer can properly claim that this would involve a departure from the concept of mutual contract implicit in the evolution of the system. Rather, it would place a special tax upon the employment of higher-salaried personnel justified only by the general taxing powers of government, with no relation to a previously assumed and proper cost of production under sound personnel policies, or to a concept of mutual contract in the terms of employment. The employer could properly argue that, as employer, he has fulfilled his obligation for the support of the system when his contributions match those of his employees, and that any additional financing required should be borne by the government through *general* taxation.

The philosophical justification of contributions to social insurance programs by employed workers and employers comes up against practical problems if implemented without compromise in the case of an important category of persons who, while needing protection, are self-employed. To require them to contribute at full rates as *both* an employer and as an employee would arouse serious opposition to compulsory coverage. Further, it might well be financially unfair. To permit them to contribute at the employee rate alone and still receive full benefits would place a heavy cost upon the social insurance system. It was not until 1950 that a compromise to this practical dichotomy was worked out. The solution was the ancient one of splitting the difference.

93

The Advisory Council of 1937-38 recommended that the self-employed be covered as soon as feasible, and that studies should be made of the administrative, legal, and financial problems involved. The Advisory Council of 1947-48, ten years later, recommended immediate coverage of the self-employed and proposed that their contribution rate should be one and one-half times the rate payable by an employee. The method of collection suggested was inclusion of the contribution in income tax returns, a method which had become available with the broadening of income tax coverage. Several reasons were given by the Council for the compromise rate. Self-employed income often included more than compensation for personal service alone. If twice the employee rate were charged, high-income self-employed persons who contributed for long periods might be "overcharged" for their coverage in relation to what they would have to pay for comparable protection under private insurance. Finally, it was recognized that self-employed persons were likely to continue to work after the normal age of retirement of persons working for an employer. For this reason, they would contribute longer and be on benefit for a shorter time. The Council's conclusion is an interesting example of the ability of such a body, through thorough discussion, to come to a creative compromise between *a priori* logic and practical considerations. The use of a simple formula, one and one-half times, gave an appearance of fairness which attempted precision would have lacked.

That practical conditions still affect the compromise in setting the contribution rate for the self-employed is indicated by the fact that slight departures from the precise formula have occurred following 1961 in avoiding odd fractions in the rate. Also, the rate for hospital insurance coverage, as a segment of the combined tax, has been set at the same percentage as for an employee alone. Even more significant is the decision, in planning future contribution rates under the system, to avoid increases in the self-employment rate after reaching 7 percent, even though the one and one-half formula would require a somewhat higher figure.

It was not until 1950, however, that self-employed persons were brought under coverage. Even then, professional workers were excluded. In 1954 and 1956, the exclusion of professional workers was narrowed, and by 1965, the last professional group, doctors of medicine, were covered as self-employed persons.

Meanwhile, the coverage of the system was being extended to many additional employed groups as political and administrative issues, rather than those of social insurance philosophy, were resolved. So far as the latter alone is the basis of policy, every gainfully employed person who faces the risk of losing earnings because of the contingencies covered by a social insurance program should be covered by the plan. Since the step-by-step extension of coverage of the OASDI program involves a long history of specific legal, political, and administrative accommodations to this basic social insurance philosophy, a discussion of them has been left to studies in these fields. An important goal toward which progress has been minimal is that of covering federal civil service employees. It also provides an outstanding example of the complex *practical* issues which can delay the implementation of a sound philosophy of universal coverage.

## CHAPTER VII

# The Issue of Financial Support of
# Social Insurance by Government

IT IS AN UNFORTUNATE PARADOX that the assumptions which led workers and progressive employers in America to accept the imposition of contributions through payroll taxes for the support of an old age insurance program have, from the first, proved to be obstacles in persuading the American people that the government should also participate in the financing of such a program. The concept of mutual benefit and social contract which had long justified contributions on the part of workers to social insurance programs encouraged many inside and outside of government to assume that social insurance was a pseudo-private insurance scheme benefiting a particular group of participants and not the country as a whole. The corollary assumption was that it should be self-financed by the group it benefited and not become a charge upon the government. To persons of this mind, the willingness of workers to pay for a specific benefit was understandable, just as with private insurance plans. Why should the government "subsidize" this particular insurance program?

The willingness of influential corporate leaders to accept payroll taxes for financing old age insurance came as a surprise to many persons in high places in Washington. The interrelations of old age insurance and corporate personnel policies were little understood. Once it was realized, however, that the corporations assumed that their contributions were a part of the cost of maintaining an effective labor force and would be passed on to the consumer, few government officials or members of Congress were inclined to support any proposal that the government join in financing the social insurance program. Employers were well able to pay and payroll taxes were a marvelous new invention in shifting costs away from the taxes most citizens resisted.

The special feature of an old age insurance program that a relatively large body of employed workers and their employers would be financing benefits for a small number of retired workers for many years to come strengthened the notion that no government financing would be needed. The understanding of actuarial costing of future benefits was almost as rare in Congress as any understanding of foreign social insurance experience. Those in government who foresaw the steadily increasing costs in future years, including Secretary Morgenthau, argued for the building of an immense reserve fund within the pseudo-private, self-supporting system in order to *avoid* any future financial participation by government. That such an immense reserve fund, both in its accumulation and its investment, created sticky problems in the fiscal operations of government failed to persuade the Secretary of the Treasury that future costs of a great national social insurance program could not be met in the same way as in a private insurance company.

The staff members of the Committee on Economic Security responsible for the planning of the old age insurance system were convinced that eventual government contributions would be necessary. To provide a reasonable level of benefits for those retiring in the early years of the system would require paying far more in benefits to the retired worker than the worker and his employer had contributed. The difference, drawn from the contributions of younger workers, would need to be reimbursed to the system as these younger workers became old. Again, to shift this burden to younger workers would require higher and higher payroll taxes as years passed. At some point, the charge upon payroll taxes would become too burdensome to be acceptable to the employees and employers paying them or in its effect upon labor costs.

In private insurance terms, the system assumed an accrued liability in paying adequate benefits to those retiring in the early years of the system. A private employer would be required to set up a fund to meet this accrued liability. The question in planning was how much of this accrued liability should be met through payroll taxes and how much through government contributions when these were needed to balance income and outgo in the system.

The solution of the problem reached by the staff was a compromise. By a gradual rise in the contribution rates, but a rise somewhat faster than current funds were needed for the payment of benefits, a modest reserve would be accumulated. When out-payments began to exceed income, many years ahead, the government would be called upon to contribute sufficiently to maintain the reserve intact. Meanwhile the reserve would serve both as a source of interest return and as a contingency reserve to meet year-by-year fluctuations between income and outgo.

It was the conviction of the staff that the accrued liability within the system was a proper charge upon the government. Millions of aged workers who would otherwise require needs-test old age pensions, entirely financed by the state and federal governments, would be receiving benefits, instead, from the contributory social insurance system. It seemed entirely reasonable to ask the government to reimburse the system the amount it would save through reduced old age assistance payments. Since the large collections from payroll taxes relative to benefit costs in the early years made early government contributions unnecessary, the obligation of the government to help meet the accrued liability could be long postponed. It is interesting to note that the staff estimated that the first government contributions would be required approximately twenty-five years after the initiation of the system, or in 1962.

The position of the planners of the old age insurance program on the staff of the Committee on Economic Security was not accepted by the Administration or the Congress in 1935. To make the program "self-sufficient," a much larger reserve was contemplated. The Advisory Council on Social Security of 1937-38, which had time to make a thorough study of the problems of financing the system, supported the early planners in calling for an eventual government contribution. Since the recommendations of the Council are as relevant today as when they were submitted, the first four of the succinctly worded statements on financing justify *verbatim* quotation:

I. Since the nation as a whole, independent of the beneficiaries of the system, will derive a benefit from the old-age security program, it is appropriate that there be Federal financial participation in the old-age insurance system by means of revenue derived from sources other than payroll taxes.

II. The principle of distributing the eventual cost of the old-age insurance system by means of approximately equal contributions by employers, employees, and the government is sound and should be definitely set forth in the law when tax provisions are amended.

III. The introduction of a definite program of Federal financial participation in the system will affect the consideration of the future rates of taxes on employers and employees and their relation to future benefit payments.

IV. The financial program of the system should embody provision for a reasonable contingency fund to insure the ready payment of benefits at all times and to avoid abrupt changes in tax and contribution rates.

In support of these findings, the Council emphasized not only the important function of old age insurance in preventing dependency in the future, but the effect of the system in reducing existing costs of old age relief and assistance. It stated that governmental participation in the financing of a social insurance had long been accepted as sound policy in other countries and that there were definite limits in the proper use of payroll taxes. In respect to the financing of the system, the Council indicated that by the introduction of government participation the difficult problem of relating tax and benefit flows without the accumulation of unwieldy reserves

100

could be far more readily resolved. The Council supported, rather, a contingency reserve, not the far larger reserve contemplated in the 1935 legislation.

The Advisory Council of 1947-48 repeated the recommendation of its predecessor that there should be financial participation by the government, and that the assumption should be that general taxation would eventually share more or less equally with employees and employers in financing future benefit outlays and administrative costs. Again, the accrued liabilities assumed by the system in relieving the government and the general taxpayer of the costs of public assistance was considered a justification of future financial participation.

Since there was no apparent need for a government contribution to the system for many years to come, after a shortlived legislative recognition of the principle from 1944 to 1950, it has been the easiest course for each successive Congress dealing with the OASDI system to avoid any reference to eventual financial participation by the government in the basic program. Transitional benefits on a minimum basis for persons already 72 and over, and not otherwise eligible for benefits, were recognized as a responsibility of the general taxpayer. This mild concession to the concept of accrued liability did not cause any serious consideration of the concept in respect to the system as a whole. The idea of a three-way sharing of the cost of OASDI seems to have disappeared from the minds of a new generation of congressmen.

The change in climate in respect to government contributions to the system was not limited to the Congress. The Advisory Council of 1957-58, which was specifically assigned the task of reviewing the financing of the

101

OASDI program, made no mention of a government contribution in its report. Instead it reverted to a solid position of justifying contributions by employers, employees, and the self-employed as the proper supporters of the system. The employee and the self-employed should contribute because they were the eventual beneficiaries; the employer, because the protection of the employee was a proper charge upon production. After almost a quarter-century, the concept of a self-financing system, which so influenced the Administration and Congress in 1935, had again become the accepted gospel.

It is of interest to speculate why American experience in the financing of social insurance has departed so sharply from that of most other countries where governmental financial participation is taken for granted. Since no one reason seems to be a sufficient explanation, several may be suggested.

1. With the remarkable increase in the efficiency of American industry and the rising level of earnings which that efficiency has supported, a majority of American workers have found that their contributions to OASDI take but a relatively small part of the increased income available for purposes beyond bare and immediate necessities. Further, the method of tax collection through payroll deductions has shifted attention from taxes to net "take-home" earnings.

2. Meanwhile, the interest of American wage-earners in programs for lifelong security have steadily increased, stimulated by the widespread impact of the OASDI program itself, as it has been improved over the years, and by broadened fringe benefit programs in industry sponsored by both employers and trade unions.

102

3. For the employer, contributions to OASDI as a universal charge on production have found their way into the normal price structure. In mass production industries where labor-saving technology has drastically reduced relative manpower costs, the cost of fringe benefits, including social insurance, has been spread over a greatly increased flow of production. The employers for whom labor costs are relatively high, as in construction or the service trades, have been under such pressure from trade unions that they have not been in a position to exercise their limited influence upon Congress in holding down payroll taxes.

4. It is not difficult to understand the passive resistance of the government to any proposals for financial participation in the basic OASDI program. In the face of immediate and gigantic expenditures for the military establishment, space development, and, more recently, for public assistance and Medicaid, a long-run obligation to meet an accrued liability in the OASDI system is easily set aside, especially by the congressional committees concerned with the general financing of government along with that of OASDI. The experts who call attention to the obligation have few votes. The slow but steady rise in payroll taxes has not yet become a concern for those who pay them and do have the votes. Actuarial science is still a mystery for most people, and the future costs of the system are something for our children to worry about.

5. Probably the most justifiable argument for postponing consideration of financial participation by government in the OASDI system is that reliance upon payroll taxes alone, even though questionable in principle, affords a political brake upon the generosity of Congress in succes-

sive election years. So long as Congress, and the Committee on Ways and Means in particular, must balance the flow of benefits with the flow of payroll taxes in the years immediately ahead, the joy of giving is somewhat restrained. The hazard in carrying this argument too far is that restraint may turn into resistance to needed improvements in the system, especially for disadvantaged groups such as the disabled or the worker of low but regular earnings. Further, it is not at all clear that those who pay progressive income taxes would object less effectively to unduly generous liberalizations in OASDI benefits than wage earners and their employers. It could be argued that, in America, social insurance has progressed faster than otherwise because it was *not* dependent upon the proceeds of progressive income taxes. The question is: Can it continue to progress in the future without a three-way sharing of steadily mounting costs?

The reasons suggested for the lack of interest in government participation in the financing of OASDI do not encourage the expectation that a shift in policy is imminent. Average earnings are still rising. Interest in lifelong security is still increasing. Industrial technology is still improving, and the federal budget is under great strain in meeting the requirements of national security and domestic progress. There are, however, two pressures at work which may force a reconsideration of policy. Both are concerned with the effectiveness of the total national social insurance program in serving the purpose for which it was intended.

The first pressure relates to the scale of benefits under OASDI. The program was intended to lift beneficiaries who have been regularly employed throughout life from the necessity of resorting to needs-test assistance. Yet the average benefits now being paid to persons regularly employed, but at *low average wages*, are less than the amounts now considered necessary under assistance programs. The lag in benefit levels, not at the minimum, but in the far more significant bracket from $100 to $200 in primary benefit, has become serious when compared to the costs of urban living today. To raise these benefits will require higher payroll taxes both in terms of percentage contribution and in the ceiling of covered earnings. With mounting payroll taxes, it is probable that employees and employers will become much more interested in government financial participation. If resistance to both higher payroll taxes and government contributions develops, the standards of OASDI protection will become eroded relative to the presumptive needs of beneficiaries and to the level of needs-test assistance.

Even if employers and employees do not effectively resist the imposition of higher and higher payroll taxes to finance the cash and hospital benefits under the social security system, there are reasons in national economic policy to spread these costs more widely. A payroll tax, whatever its eventual purpose, is a tax on the use of labor. To the employer, it is a direct cost even though passed on, whenever possible, to the consumer. Because of the concern of the employee in his "take-home" pay, there is pressure where the bargaining power exists, for organized workers to shift the cost of their social insurance contributions to the employer and through him to the consumer. The result of these combined effects, especially if payroll taxes reach critical importance in costs of production, is to accentuate the shift to labor-saving methods. In some

105

industries, this is readily possible with a concomitant curtailment of jobs. In other industries, where human service is heavily involved and labor-saving methods are not available, the product or service may come to bear such heavy additional costs of shifted payroll taxes that its market is reduced. The avoidance of this effect in distorting a national economy requires a balancing of the means of financing a social security program through the use of more general taxes, and not payroll taxes alone.

The second pressure which may cause a change in financial policy is that for a more comprehensive pattern of social insurance benefits. Already, the introduction of Medicare insurance has required a considerable increase in the combined rate of payroll taxes. There is strong reason to believe that the costs of Medicare, even without a change in coverage, will continue to increase. If coverage is extended to primary beneficiaries of the disability insurance program, a sharp increase in costs will occur. An extension of Medicare protection to dependents under both the survivorship and the disability programs would further add to costs. Even for the aged, alone, there is reason to consider the broadening of benefits to cover, in part at least, the cost of out-of-hospital drugs.

These and other improvements in the federal social insurance program would, if introduced, encourage a serious reconsideration of the methods of financing the program. Further, the charging of monthly premiums for Part B of Medicare was a makeshift from the first. To ask aged beneficiaries voluntarily to accept deductions from benefits, regardless of their adequacy, to obtain essential medical services seems inconsistent with sound social in-

106

surance policy. The inevitable increases in the rates of premiums will make the shortcomings of this method of financing even more obvious. Meanwhile, the matching of Part B Medicare premiums by government contributions has established the principle of such contributions to one element of a social insurance system at the cost of splitting apart what should be a single, integrated program.

There is reason to expect that the reopening of the issue of government participation in the social insurance program as a whole will result, in first instance, from the need to expand Medicare in both its scope and pattern of benefits. There are special reasons for this conclusion.

1. The accrued liability assumed by the Medicare system at its initiation in covering millions of persons already old is so large and obvious that the obligation of government to help meet it is evident. Why should payroll taxes alone bear this accrued cost when the parallel costs for Medicaid are entirely met from government appropriations? Workers in the younger age groups, along with their employers, are relieving the general taxpayer whenever an older person on Medicare would otherwise be eligible for Medicaid.

2. Unlike OASDI, with its graduated benefits related to past earnings, Medicare provides the same protection for the beneficiary who has contributed the minimum sufficient for eligibility as for the beneficiary who has contributed at the maximum for many years. This degree of social redistribution of the costs involved may be questioned when the only source of funds is payroll taxes. Government participation in the financing of Medicare

as a total system, and not in Part B alone, would greatly help in justifying this redistribution of costs. Through the use of progressive income taxes to meet a part of the costs, the generosity of government in providing medical care for low-income citizens would be balanced by responsibility on the part of government in paying its share of the bill. By assuring the continued acceptance of a social insurance approach to health care, the government will prevent a persistent drift to relief and public medicine.

3. Medicare benefits differ from cash benefits in the degree of control on the part of the beneficiary over the costs, once illness has occurred. The recipient of an OASDI payment receives a fixed sum which he can use as he sees fit. The service rendered under Medicare is determined in each case by physicians and hospital administrations, more directly, and by governmental agencies and policies, indirectly. The government is an important factor in the support and control of health services through the financing of hospital construction, medical education, and medical research. The support of an important method of assuring effective *delivery* of health services—social insurance—is but a small step beyond those already taken. For the government to help build the hospital, to help educate the doctor, and to advance medical research, but to stick at helping to make good health care more readily available to the aged patient as an earned right, seems shortsighted and inconsistent. With the government as a partner in the financing of Medicare, it would be encouraged to assume leadership in the rationalization of the whole system of *distribution* of medical care. Such leadership has become the essential but

108

lacking ingredient in any major improvement in the effectiveness of health care in the United States.

The United States Government has come to a time of decision in choosing whether it will throw its major support to needs-test Medicaid or to contributory social insurance—Medicare—in meeting its recognized obligation to assure adequate medical services for those who can no longer pay for them because of age, survivorship, or disability. By emphasizing the path of needs-test assistance after self-reliance has been undermined, it will incur increasing costs in both dollar and social terms. By supporting more effectively the method of contributory social insurance, it will make more orderly and rational the financing of a great and growing service to its citizens and, at the same time, preserve and enhance the precious attributes of self-reliance and incentive in our society.

The general conclusion on the issue of financial support by government of a social insurance system seems clear. There are sound reasons in both social insurance philosophy and general economic policy for the sharing of the costs of the total system on a three-way basis, as the Advisory Council of 1937-38 recommended. Time has not lessened, but rather strengthened, the force of the Council's position. Habits of mind and political resistance, however, make a *general* application of the principle of three-way financing unlikely for some time to come. But there are urgent and, it is to be hoped, more convincing reasons for its application in one segment of the system, Medicare. Since the payroll taxes for OASDI and Hospital Insurance are merged in their assessment on the employer and employee, the three-way financing of Hos-

109

pital Insurance would moderate the rise in the total pay-roll charge. Even better would be the three-way financing of the *whole* Medicare program, eliminating the unfortunate historical accident of a monthly premium for voluntary coverage under Part B charged upon old people when they are least able to pay it.

## CHAPTER VIII

# General Issues in Respect to the Contingencies
# Covered under Social Insurance

IN ORDER TO DETERMINE the contingencies against
which social insurance can effectively provide protection, it is necessary to define the essential elements of the
mechanism. First, under social insurance as a form of *insurance*, there must be an insurable risk, that is, something concrete and definite which is lost under conditions
beyond the control of the insured. Both the thing lost and
the fact of loss must be clearly ascertainable and susceptible to actuarial estimate. In the area of human experience normally associated with social insurance, the things
insured against are the loss of earnings previously available through gainful employment or the loss of health of
persons who were previously normally employed and who
require medical services to regain their health. In the
former case, the indemnification of loss is in the form of
a cash benefit; in the latter case, it can be in the form
of health services in kind or in the reimbursement of the
cost of such services to the insured person.

As *social* insurance, rather than private indemnity insurance, several additional qualifications are normal. The
need for protection by insurance is deemed to be so widespread that a governmental body sponsors and adminis-
ters the program. Further, in justification of government
sponsorship, the design of the program is one emphasizing imputed need on the part of those protected as
compared to individual equity on a *quid pro quo* basis.

111

This permits a degree of adjustment in eligibility requirements for all benefits and in the relationship of cash benefits to previous earnings which implements social considerations. Further, the emphasis upon imputed need involves the extension of the protection afforded from the primary beneficiary, whose earnings or health are lost, to those assumed to be or to have been dependent upon him and his earnings. Social insurance, if it requires contributions from its potential beneficiaries, must also recognize that its acceptance arises from a sense of social contract for mutual protection and, therefore, must assure a structure of benefits deemed a fair return by most participants.

From this somewhat oversimplified description of the essential characteristics of social insurance, it is relatively easy to indicate the areas and conditions of human need for which it is *not* an appropriate means of protection. A person who has, through lifelong mental or physical disability, been unfitted for gainful employment cannot be insured against the loss of earnings which he has never had. He may, as a dependent of a parent who is eligible because of gainful employment, become a secondary beneficiary when the parent for reasons of old age, disability, or death is no longer able to support him.

As a matter of degree, a person whose earnings through gainful employment are determined to be insufficient to serve as evidence of an insurable risk may be properly excluded from eligibility for benefit under social insurance as a primary beneficiary. The borderline in this case involves considerations of principle, social policy, and administrative effectiveness. As embodying a sense of social contract, the contribution of the marginal partici-

112

pant under social insurance may be too small in either economic or financial terms to warrant fulfillment of contract at the expense of other contributors to the program. Further, the probable need of the marginal participant is so much greater than the protection which social insurance can reasonably provide that another method of protection, needs-test public assistance, is socially preferable. Finally, the administrative costs of providing such a minimal degree of protection through social insurance payments may be out of reasonable proportion to the protection afforded.

A more difficult area in delimiting the appropriate role of social insurance is that in which the incidence of an insurable contingency cannot be clearly defined. It is far easier to determine that a potential beneficiary is 65 years old and without earnings than that, at 55, his lack of earnings is the result of a weak back and not a weakened motivation to work. All insurance is faced with the problem of moral risk where the incidence of the contingency, in the absence of objective evidence of cause, arises out of a subjective predisposition on the part of the claimant favorable to its occurrence. An advantage in the administration of old age and survivorship insurance is that age and death are physical phenomena. At the other extreme, unemployment insurance must depend upon means of determining when a person is able, available, and *motivated* to seek employment. Disability and health insurance straddle a wide span of contingencies from those obvious to any observer to those requiring the expert judgment of panels of physicians.

It is of interest that in the almost parallel development of two major types of social insurance in the United

States, old age insurance and unemployment insurance, the former dealing with a readily definable contingency, old age and a major loss of earnings from employment, has progressed smoothly with widespread acceptance. The latter, unemployment insurance, dealing at the borderline of eligibility for benefit with the subjective attitudes of the beneficiary toward employment, has been the subject of continuing criticism based upon much-exaggerated reports of abuses. Only by the most careful administration have the more recent forms of social insurance, long-term disability and Medicare, avoided any serious question of abuse on the part of beneficiaries. The degree of objectivity which can be exercised in the determination of the incidence or continuance of the covered contingency is a very real consideration in the extension of the scope of social insurance.

A further consideration in building a system of social insurance is whether the loss or cost involved in the incidence of the contingency is sufficiently serious in its impact upon the person covered to warrant the intervention of the government. For example, many years elapsed after the introduction of old age insurance in the United States before the Congress was convinced that older persons dependent on social insurance benefits could not meet the rising costs of medical services without a further form of social insurance—Medicare. The need to insure old age insurance beneficiaries against the cost of drugs for out-of-hospital use is still being debated. There has been a general assumption that most persons in their working years can absorb the cost of needed health services within their current income, either directly or through premiums paid under private forms of insurance. The question at

114

issue now is whether, without the mechanism of compulsory contributory social insurance, with its attributes of social redistribution and a broader base of financing, including government participation, far too many lower-income workers are unable to protect themselves by private mechanisms.

In the chapters which follow, the several areas and aspects of the American social security program, as it now exists, will be analyzed in order to indicate the philosophical principles and the practical considerations which have influenced the evolution of that element of the total program. Many of the issues in philosophy and policy, as they affect each element, have been resolved over the years. Others have been brought to a stage of reasonable compromise in the face of many countervailing factors. Still others remain to be solved if that element of the total system is to attain the degree of effectiveness and scope which will balance progress and security for the American people. But the whole is greater than its parts. The total social security system, like a great and growing oak, must develop as an integrated whole and, to do so, it must at the same time strengthen its roots and trunk, as well as its branches. In discussing the various features of the system, therefore, this interrelation of the fundamental concepts which support the whole structure must be constantly kept in mind.

## CHAPTER IX

# The Determination of the Contingency to be Covered under Old Age Insurance

SINCE 1935, when social insurance was instituted to indemnify the loss of earnings because of age, it has been expanded to cover wives, widows, widowers, children, and dependent parents of primary beneficiaries under prescribed conditions. The established *normal* age of eligibility—that is, the age at which full benefits are provided—remains 65, but eligibility for reduced benefits has moved down from 65 to 62 for primary beneficiaries and their wives. Widows are now eligible for a full widow's benefit at 62 and a reduced benefit at 60. Disabled widows or disabled, dependent widowers may receive reduced benefits, based upon a primary beneficiary's record, as early as age 50.

The most significant element in defining the contingency to be covered under old age insurance is the *normal* age at which benefits should become available. Is age 65 a reasonable norm for establishing the time in life when most workers shift from gainful employment sufficient for self-support to a condition of dependency upon means of support apart from current earnings from employment? The selection of age 65 in the 1935 Act was a matter of judgment based upon practice under industrial pension plans at home and social insurance programs abroad. The various revisions made since 1935 in the age at which old age insurance benefits are payable reflect the continuing effort of the Social Security Administration,

116

periodic Advisory Councils, and the Congress to move from an arbitrary, *a priori* setting of the age of entitlement to benefits to a pattern of requirements and adjustments which is more sensitive to the actual working-life experience of our people.

Throughout this evolution of policy, it has been necessary to keep two fundamental factors in mind: (1) the age of eligibility as a powerful factor in determining costs, unless actuarial discounts are applied, and (2) the influence of the normal retirement age as established by the system upon the shift of national potentially productive manpower from full-time employment to part-time employment or retirement. The interaction between an old age insurance system and patterns of retirement involves an ever-changing complex of forces combining economic, political, and psychological factors. In the development of policy it is important to distinguish between the existence and the precise setting of a norm, on the one hand, and the various means provided for permitting individuals to depart from that norm, on the other. Social insurance requires that the insurable risk involve a concrete and definite loss, in this case earnings, under conditions which are clearly ascertainable and susceptible to actuarial estimate. In old age insurance, the insurance system must, therefore, be financially structured about a *normal* age of eligibility even though carefully controlled departures from the norm are introduced to afford flexibility.

Recent studies by the Social Security Administration indicate conclusively that retirement as a contingency in an individual's working life falls within a period of years and not at a particular year of life. For some, the shift from regular employment to partial employment or none at all occurs well before age 62. For a much larger proportion than was anticipated, the shift is a gradual alteration in the balance between employment and non-employment affected by many conditions related to personal health, diverse occupations, employment compared to self-employment, availability of jobs, financial resources, personal attitudes and, not least of all, the eligibility provisions of the old age insurance system. The zone during which this shifting balance occurs that is most significant in old age insurance policy spreads from the early to the late 60's.

The only satisfactory way to adjust a costly insurance mechanism to this pattern of retirement is by the method of neutralizing the effect of the variable element, age at retirement *before* the established norm, by providing benefits for the full retirement period following early retirement precisely equivalent in actuarial terms to the benefits otherwise provided at the established normal age. Without complete adherence to this principle, the financial and actuarial problems become awesome. Without the anchor of a fixed normal age and actuarial discounts for earlier eligibility, the system becomes caught in the powerful cross-currents of political and economic forces. What started as a system of old age insurance becomes an amorphous program of supplementing low wages in later life. Not only would difficulties arise in assuring adequate benefits, but the manpower policies of the country would become confused.

It may be suggested that an actuarial discounting of benefit amounts on early retirement should be balanced by an actuarial increment in benefit scale for late retirement *after* 65. This has been proposed from time to time. The objection, which is reasonable, is based upon the overall purpose of the old age insurance system: to prevent dependency in old age. The person who has the advantage of continuing earnings through employment beyond 65 gains the advantage of supplementing his benefits, so far as permitted by an earnings-test, or of raising his eventual benefit level by the improvement of his average wage base through the substitution of years of higher earnings. By age 72, he is eligible under OASDI to receive his old age benefits regardless of earnings through employment. In terms of the purpose of a social insurance system and the relative adequacy of the protection afforded, there seems little social justification for an actuarial supplementation because of postponement of retirement.

Whatever adjustments are made in the age at which benefits are available, the question remains: Is 65 the proper age for normal retirement and for full benefit around which to build an old age insurance system in the United States? To lower the normal age of retirement reflected in the system would require a consensus that a lower chronological age had become the primary, critical cause for the contingency of loss of normal earnings for a majority of potential beneficiaries, as distinct from secondary factors, more or less related to age, and which appropriately fall within the province of other social insurance programs, public assistance, private initiative, or remedial public programs of various kinds. Among these secondary factors which may be age-related, but do not necessarily justify a change in the established retirement

119

age in an old age insurance system, as such, are those related to disability and those related to economic conditions affecting employment.

That the incidence of disability increases with age is
universally recognized. That it should lower the established retirement age of 65 for all beneficiaries is highly
questionable. The special problems in determining disability sufficient for benefit payment under social insurance
strongly support a clear differentiation between the compensation of loss of earnings because of disability as distinct from that related to chronological age. Under disability insurance, the focus in determining the onset of
the contingency is an accurate judgment on the physical
condition of each individual against standards which can
never be explicit in every detail. The social insurance administrator must rely upon professionally certified medical evidence which justifies non-availability for work.
This emphasis upon the individual and his individually
determined condition introduces a range of discretion exercised by thousands of third-party professional experts.
This administrative process is profoundly different from
the determination of chronological age and the loss of
all, or that part of, earnings permitting eligibility. Disability insurance will always involve constant emphasis
upon close administrative controls at the point of incidence of the contingency covered. Old age insurance can
be elaborately programmed for highly centralized administration since chronological age and earnings in covered
employment are, for the vast majority of individuals,
readily determinable within the system and subject to
precise evaluation in objective terms.

To allow old age insurance to merge into disability

insurance by a process of legislative and administrative corrosion of the concept of retirement because of chronological age would be costly in social, economic, financial, and administrative terms. It would be far better to attack head-on the problem of disability in the years before 65 by refinements in the disability insurance program, despite all its special difficulties in administration, than to confuse it with old age insurance. The lowering of the established chronological age for full benefits under old age insurance would be a costly makeshift. It would never solve the social problem involved since disability can occur at any age. That men become unemployed more often as disability is compounded by age is not the issue. The true issue is what form of social insurance is best in providing needed protection. A small degree of flexibility about an established chronological retirement age, with tight actuarial controls, is possible in old age insurance, but this is no proper substitute for an adequate program of disability insurance.

The other secondary factor which may suggest departure from the proper delimitation of the function of old age insurance with its need for an established chronological retirement age is the higher incidence of unemployment among *able-bodied*, older persons. The great diversity of causes for such unemployment, apart from age, suggests that a wide diversity of remedies is required. Unemployment may be seasonal, cyclical, or technological; general or sporadic; related to particular areas, industries, or skills (or lack of them); it may involve persons normally employed by firms or self-employed, or arise from shifting life patterns, incentives, or relative affluence. The fact that more *older* people may be affected

121

by these conditions does not alter the fact that the primary causes for unemployment among any category of workers, old or young, urban or rural, white or black, are highly diverse. Therefore, the instrumentalities for preventing unemployment or alleviating the condition of those affected must be highly diverse.

Among the public mechanisms for the prevention or alleviation of the incidence of loss of earnings through unemployment are national fiscal policy, central banking controls, planned public works, support of industrial rehabilitation in specific areas, employment services, retraining programs, unemployment insurance, and public assistance. Constructive national policy involves all these and more, for all persons needing work, and not older workers alone. More particularly for the old, a limited social insurance benefit, if it implies early and permanent displacement from normal self-sufficiency through wanted work, is a poor substitute for broad and dynamic social policy. To the extent that other measures fail and unemployment insurance benefits are exhausted, reliance must be placed upon a greatly improved public assistance program which will protect older displaced workers until they are eligible for old age insurance benefits at an established age, just as it protects younger workers for the period of their need. Old age insurance cannot be made the crutch for a limping economy and still perform its proper function effectively. That it works well in performing its own specific function is no excuse for stretching it to cover shortcomings in national economic policy or for making it take the place of the undergirding structure of an effective national system of public assistance.

Not only would the lowering of the established retirement age under old age insurance condone lack of foresight and vigor on the part of government in economic and manpower policy, but it would also condone the failure of private employers to use our human resources effectively. With the growth of large, perpetual, corporations, the problem of displacement of superannuated workers or those with obsolete skills has become a matter of both concern and cost. With the accelerating change in technology, many employers would profit if they could avoid any responsibility to match the pattern of their labor forces in terms of age to the age distribution of generally qualified workers now employed or now available in their community. A young worker and a new machine may combine to enhance profits. The old machine may be displaced with an accounting adjustment merely. The early displacement of an older worker, however, involves a complex of social and economic factors within the corporation, within the community, and within the country. Fortunately, the institutional resistances to arbitrary, profit-centered practices in displacing older employees are still strong in America.

It is not the employer alone who might take advantage of the lowering of the established retirement age under old age insurance in a manner contrary to sound national manpower policy. Trade unions in which younger men predominate might, especially in time of decreasing demand, be willing to accept contract terms which would accelerate the displacement of older workers, using the excuse of partial compensation under old age insurance. Even though such compensation were supplemented by other payments, there would be a loss to society of the productivity of still effective manpower. The granting of

123

the "privilege" of early retirement can be made to appear a generous policy until those forced to accept the privilege find that long-continuing leisure on reduced income is less satisfying than advertised to be. There should be better ways to adjust the factors of supply and demand in terms of national human resources than by putting the social and economic cost of maladjustment on the older worker alone.

By establishing age 65 as the normal age of retirement, the Social Security Act both reflected and reinforced existing corporate policy. A decision by the United States Government to lower this normal age would have long-continuing influence on thousands of employers and many unions in justifying, at a time of rapid technological change, the earlier displacement of millions of older workers from the employment which now contributes to their own wellbeing and that of the nation. But efficiency for the individual firm or the interest of a single union is too narrow a focus for the determination of a national manpower policy. The established retirement age under OASDI is a significant element in national manpower policy. It involves social as well as economic values. Participation in productive enterprise is a source of human satisfaction for which dollars alone are but a limited substitute. It may seem generous to ameliorate the early loss of employment in the individual situation, but it is far more beneficial in human terms to lessen the risk of early displacement for all.

The time may come when widespread affluence encourages a preference for retirement and leisure before 65 among a large segment of the American people. This is their choice to make. Since affluence is presumed to eliminate the need for social insurance protection, early retirement can be financed by individual arrangements. Yet old age insurance will still be needed for those less fortunate and for those who misjudge their future needs. There is no justification for the government to make early retirement a little more attractive to those who have sufficient private means and private mechanisms to support a voluntary choice.

While the established age for normal retirement is a fundamental issue in social security policy, it has not received the attention in recent years which another issue, the earnings-test, has gained. The contingency to be covered by old age insurance is not age alone but insufficient earnings from current employment *because of old age.* Old age insurance is indemnity insurance. It is the non-existence of any earnings from employment, or of sufficient earnings for reasonable support, which is indemnified. This aspect of the contingency to be compensated has been the focus of more misunderstanding since the Social Security Act was passed than any other feature of old age insurance. There is a strong tendency to confuse benefits under social insurance with prepaid annuities under private insurance. The sharp distinctions in purpose, form, and financing are but dimly recognized by most workers. Even members of Congress have been known to have some difficulty in explaining this aspect of social insurance to their constituents.

It was soon discovered in the development of the old age insurance program that the contingency of loss of earnings must be determined in terms of imputed need just as a scale of benefits is developed in terms of imputed need. It began to be recognized that "retirement" for age

125

often involved not a clean-cut withdrawal from all gainful employment but a shifting balance from regular employment to degrees of part-time employment. Those who needed insurance protection most were most likely to seek ways to supplement their lower-than-average benefits.

Unlike a scale of benefits which is related to average earnings in a prescribed past period, a determination of permissible earnings while on benefit must, for both social and administrative reasons, be related to *current* earnings, year by year or month by month. The only practical way to administer an earnings-test appears to be a fixed schedule of allowances or offsets applied uniformly in all cases so that all beneficiaries can adjust their employment accordingly, if they so desire. The social advantage of the fixed offset method is that the combination of benefits and earnings resulting can be readily related to a socially determined amount based on imputed living costs. Unlike private retirement annuities, social insurance does not need to recognize the full loss of earnings on retirement, but rather that degree of loss which is socially undesirable.

The history of the earnings-test for eligibility for full or partial benefits under OASDI is that of a long process of gradual liberalization. The 1935 Act eliminated benefits if any wages were received in any month in regular employment. This loose restriction was changed in 1939 to a provision that monthly earnings less than $15.00 would be disregarded. From 1950 to 1958, the disregarded monthly amount was gradually increased to $100. By 1960, a new device of a zone in which but one-half of the earned amount would be disregarded was added.

By then the schedule of offsets had become $100 in any month, $1,200 in a year, plus one-half of the amount earned between $1,200 and $1,500. By 1967, this had been raised to $140 in any month, $1,680 in a year, plus one-half of the amount earned between $1,680 and $2,880. Further revisions were under consideration in 1971.

This history of gradual adjustment confirms the premise that any earnings-test must embody a practical balancing of several considerations in contributory social insurance system. First is the basic consideration that old age insurance is intended to prevent dependency and hardship in old age. It cannot afford to divert a large flow of funds to persons still normally employed who have no special need for benefit. For them the contingency of loss of normal earnings through employment has not arisen. Therefore, the extreme position of eliminating an earnings-test departs from sound social insurance principles. Further, the elimination of an earnings-test would divert funds from a higher priority in protecting our citizens to a far lower priority, since persons continuing in normal employment, even though old, need protection far less than those incurring the contingencies as yet inadequately covered.

At the other extreme, a disqualification from benefits because of earnings which is too restrictive or too rigid flies in the face of the conditions which surround for many workers the transition from regular employment to complete retirement. Old age insurance benefits, at best, provide but a partial replacement of regular wage income. To foreclose gain from supplementary earnings not only holds down the living standard of the beneficiary, but displaces him with arbitrary finality from the normal system of incentive and reward under which he has lived throughout life. The changes which come with old age are unsettling enough without sudden removal of the satisfaction of some gainful work.

The issue becomes not total disqualification but how much gainful employment should be disregarded and still provide all or a part of the benefit available on complete retirement. As earlier suggested, the actual schedule of allowances must be in dollars, since the policy planner, the administrator, and the beneficiary, each for his own reason, must convert broad considerations into an exact and understandable basis for decision. Social policy, administrative effectiveness, and the way of life of millions of beneficiaries are all involved in the precise balance attained.

Experience over the years has shown that some flexibility in an earnings-test formula goes far in matching an apparently arbitrary rule to the work patterns of older people. A disregarded amount, such as $2,000 a year with a reduction in benefits by one-half of any earnings above $2,000, avoids the harshness of a sharp line of demarcation between entire gain and no gain in income when a beneficiary secures part-time employment. It is not always easy for the beneficiary to keep an up-to-date record of past earnings within the year and to adjust plans for further work in later months. The counsel of perfection would be for an older person to disregard the earnings-test if jobs were available. As a practical matter, however, not all earnings are a net gain, since there are expenses associated with employment as well as taxes and other deductions.

Another means of reducing the rigidity of an earnings-test is to eliminate it entirely after a fixed age, such as 72. By this time of life but a small minority of older persons are continuing in normal employment. Many of this minority are in self-employment and have contributed for seven additional years to old age insurance after most have retired. Although meanwhile protected, they have received no cash return. Even for those who have received partial or interrupted benefits in the intervening period from 65 to 72, the total elimination of offsets after 72 helps in sustaining a sense of reward for years of contribution throughout one's working life. Contributory social insurance must reflect in its operations the sense of social contract which is one of its appeals. A contract which may never pay out, even though one is unusually fortunate, loses something of its charm.

The American program of old age insurance has now evolved over a third of a century in its philosophy, policies, and administration. So far as the determination of the contingency it seeks to cover is concerned, it appears to be approaching a mature state. The normal age of eligibility of 65 has stood the test for years. Earlier eligibility to permit flexibility has been controlled by preserving approximate actuarial equivalence. The earnings-test has been gradually liberalized over the years to reflect rising living costs and an increased understanding of the diverse conditions surrounding retirement. The pressures for further change in the determination of the *contingency* to be covered by old age insurance appear to arise out of the shortcomings in the development of other programs for social security or manpower utilization rather than out of shortcomings within the old age insurance program as a distinct form of social insurance. There are other issues concerning the program, however, including benefit structure, benefit levels, and financing which are considered elsewhere.

## CHAPTER X

# The Coverage of Dependents and Survivors

NO ASPECT OF the early history of the American social security program illustrates more clearly the climate of desperate urgency in which the old age staff of the Committee on Economic Security labored in the fall of 1934 than the absence in the original Social Security Act of any effective social insurance mechanism for protecting the dependents or survivors of those covered under old age insurance. Time was short and the staff minuscule. A radical innovation, contributory social insurance, had to be sold to the Administration and Congress as a proper instrumentality of the national government. Issues related to constitutionality, the appropriate level of administration, and financing were desperately acute and had to be resolved in a few short weeks. Since the Congress faced a rapidly mounting pressure to establish a system of free pensions such as demanded by millions of distressed old people throughout the country, it was understandable that the staff focused its major attention on planning a constructive mechanism for the protection of the aged. The critical challenge was to establish the concept of contributory social insurance in national policy to lift vast numbers off needs-test relief. If the concept was established, refinements in implementation of the social insurance approach could come later.

Under these conditions, the original planners of the old age insurance program settled for a return of contributions on the death of the insured person. An early trial draft in September, 1934, proposed that "all contributions [both employers' and employees'] shall be paid with interest to the wife, husband, or dependent child or parent of the insured . . ." if the deceased person had drawn no benefits. If some benefits had been paid, the remaining balance in his account should be returned. It was suggested that while a small survivor benefit might be socially desirable where pension payments had begun, it would add materially to the actuarial cost of the plan. The strategic opportunity to develop a closely interlocking system of protection for both the aged and for dependent survivors of all ages was submerged under a cloud of anxiety that even a streamlined plan dealing with the aged alone might fail of enactment or of court approval. With so much at stake, it was not a time to add complicating refinements which would add to costs and relate benefits too closely with contributions.

The Social Security Act of 1935 called for a death benefit equivalent to 3½ percent of the total wages earned by the insured under the program should he die before benefits were paid, or the remainder of this amount if benefits had been paid. It was believed necessary for constitutional reasons to avoid any direct interlocking of contributions and benefits. The 3½ percent figure was arbitrarily determined as roughly approximately the return of joint contributions with interest, at least in the early years of the plan. It was, at best, a makeshift, crying for replacement when conditions were favorable for a comprehensive revision of the plan.

From the signing of the Act by President Roosevelt in August, 1935, to the establishment of its constitutionality, the future of the program was still uncertain. The staff of the Social Security Board was heavily engaged in solving administrative problems. Since at that time no benefits were to be paid until 1942, emphasis was placed on the machinery for collections and record-keeping. Revisions in benefit structure had to await the degree to which the Supreme Court decision sanctioned the development of a fully integrated social insurance mechanism. With the broadly based decision of the Court in May, 1937, however, the mood of those concerned with the planning of contributory old age insurance suddenly shifted from selling a radical but stripped-down innovation to the perfecting of a balanced, integrated system of protection.

The seeds of change had been planted three months before in February, 1937, when, as earlier discussed, the Senate Finance Committee agreed to appoint a special committee to cooperate with the Social Security Board in appointing an Advisory Council on Social Security to study the old age insurance titles of the Act. The Council was not appointed until May, 1937, and did not meet until November. The terms of reference outlined in the appointment of the Council are indicative of the broadening interest in the program. The Council was to consider the following matters:

(1) The advisability of commencing payment of monthly benefits under Title II sooner than January 1, 1942;

(2) The advisability of increasing the monthly benefits payable under Title II for those retiring in the early years;

(3) The advisability of extending the benefits in Title II to persons who become incapacitated prior to age 65;

133

(4) The advisability of extending the benefits of Title II to survivors of individuals entitled to such benefits;

(5) The advisability of increasing the taxes less rapidly under Title VIII;

(6) The advisability of extending the benefits under Title II to include groups now excluded;

(7) The size, character and disposition of reserves;

(8) Any other questions concerning the Social Security Act about which either the Special Senate Committee or the Social Security Board may desire the advice of the Advisory Council.

The fourth item in the list of matters to be studied was somewhat ambiguous. While a narrow interpretation could suggest that only the survivors of *retired* beneficiaries were meant—for example, widows—there was good reason to study the protection of survivors of *potential* beneficiaries, even though in mid-life. Item (2) also gave the Council a justifiable basis for expanding the *structure* of benefits in order to enhance the degree of protection in the early years. A key to the concern of the Senate Finance Committee is found, however, in items (1) and (5). The new magic of a broad-based payroll tax had become recognized. Collections would soon outstrip benefits to such an extent that unless something was done, large reserves would accumulate while potential beneficiaries waited and then received minimal amounts.

In contrast to the old age staff of the Committee on Economic Security in 1934-35, the Advisory Council on Social Security in 1937-38 faced a firm constitutional base for an integrated social insurance system; an established source of funds that suggested early expansion of the benefit structure rather than most cautious economy; and the opportunity for extensive study and deliberation with adequate staff support. The time had come for a thoroughgoing revision of the program.

The 1937-38 Advisory Council recommended many changes. In respect to the coverage of dependents and survivors, the subject of this chapter, the changes recommended were drastic. The Council proposed that a 50 percent "supplementary allowance" be paid on behalf of an aged wife (65 or over) of an eligible aged beneficiary, based on his benefit. A plain indication that this was considered a dependent's *allowance* in the form of a guaranteed underwriting and not a true benefit was the proviso that should a wife, after attaining age 65, become eligible for a *benefit* in her own right larger than the wife's allowance payable to her husband on her behalf, the benefit payable to her in her own right should be substituted for the wife's allowance. In the light of subsequent developments, it is important to note that the supplementary allowance was to be paid to the husband on behalf of a wife. The Council thus distinguished between an individual benefit right and an allowance to protect a family unit.

The Council's approach to the expansion of the old age insurance program to cover dependents and survivors is illustrated by the proposed protection for the wife. The focus of its concern was on the *family* unit. The measure of its concern was the *adequacy* of the protection afforded, not any concept of bookkeeping equity in balancing contributions and benefits. This was a highly sig-

135

nificant departure from the conceptual base of the benefit features of the 1935 Act. While some degree of graduation in benefits to the aged worker was implicit in the benefit formula in the original legislation, the return of payments on the death of the covered worker carried over a notion of equity usually associated with a private savings scheme.

It can be said that the Advisory Council of 1937-38 shifted the whole concept of what became the OASDI program from a hybrid compromise between private savings and social insurance to a clearcut concept of social insurance. The new focus became *adequacy* and the protection of the family unit. The principle of differential graduations in the primary benefits related to earnings levels was confirmed, not only to sustain incentive, but also to reflect the fact that adequacy of protection, itself, is related to the customary costs and standards of living of the family. Adequacy, not equity, was the primary consideration.

This clarification of philosophy and purpose in the American social security program consummated over thirty years ago is still not fully appreciated by some groups. So long as social and private insurance exist side by side, there will be some tendency to confuse the two. The principle of adequacy of protection justifies the wife's allowance, as well as payments to surviving widows, dependent widowers, children, and parents. The single person, man or woman, gets less for his or her contributions than the person with dependents because he is assumed to need less protection. Few people object to the concept of adequacy in determining the protection of survivors. But in more recent years the notion of equity has reappeared in an expressed grievance on behalf of working wives that they are subject to relative deprivation of rights as compared to wives who do not earn taxable wages and yet receive a wife's allowance on retirement. The argument runs that if non-working wives get "something for nothing," i.e. a 50 percent allowance, working wives should get that 50 percent allowance plus an additional benefit related to their earnings.

The answer to the complaint of the working wife goes to the heart of the concept of adequacy. The wife's allowance is based upon the need to protect the family unit whether the wife earns outside wages or not. The family unit is a basic social and economic feature of our way of life. The contribution of the wife in the home is not measurable by cash wages. Yet to deprive her of protection because her work is not directly measurable in dollars would leave millions of families with inadequate protection. If social insurance benefits were related to *cash* contributions only and not also to *economic* contribution throughout life, all beneficiaries today would receive a minor fraction of what they in fact receive. The argument of equity, if carried to its logical conclusion, reduces a social insurance program to the limited purposes of private insurance.

But, it is argued, if the wife earns wages, why can't she add the benefits which would be related to those wages on top of the wife's allowance? The answer is that this introduces a concept of equity carried over from private insurance to the unique and special advantage of one class of persons, wage-earning wives, at the expense of all other persons protected under the system, including single women. The wife, as such, as a vital element in the

137

family unit, is protected by an allowance, an underwriting that she will be protected to an adequate degree. If she departs from the role of a dependent wife who is contributing her services only through the family unit, it is reasonable that she be considered an independent worker, like her unmarried sister, eligible to a primary benefit in her own right. Under OASDI provisions she then receives several valuable forms of protection as a primary beneficiary if she meets minimum eligibility requirements. These include disability, survivorship, and retirement benefits in her own right. But she cannot add primary benefit rights as an independent wage-earner on top of a minimum *guarantee* of a wife's allowance as a special case of double protection. That would be adding apples and oranges. A worker guaranteed by contract an established minimum rate does not expect *both* the minimum rate *and* his actual earnings, including the minimum amount, as well. As years pass, a larger proportion of married women will attain benefits exceeding their wife's allowance, and the distinction between a guarantee and a primary benefit will become clearer.

Apart from its social justification, the introduction of a wife's allowance served the purpose of balancing collections and disbursements in the long-run financing of old age insurance. The benefit formula in the 1935 Act had a built-in effect of sharply accentuating the rise in disbursements over the years since benefits were to be based on the *accumulated* earnings of the beneficiary during his period of coverage. The change to an *average* earnings base, which will be discussed elsewhere, and the addition of the 50 percent wife's allowance, increased both individual and total payments immediately. Since

138

the proportion of beneficiaries with wives would remain fairly constant, the increase in disbursements on their behalf would rise no faster than primary benefits rose. Therefore, added protection could be given immediately without accentuating the acceleration in the rise of future disbursements. Thus the total effect of the wife's allowance, as well as of survivors' benefits, was to help match the income and outgo of the system, year by year, as compared to the 1935 plan. The Council's recommendations combined to improve both the social effect and the financial rationale of the system.

The question might be asked: Why did the Advisory Council hit upon 50 percent as the wife's allowance? In the recollection of the chairman of the Council, no other percentage was discussed. It was a common-sense judgment and not the result of elaborate studies. "Fifty percent" possessed a quality which might be termed "aesthetic logic" in that it looked right. Any other percentage would have seemed awkward and have encouraged debate. The fact that the 50 percent figure has never been challenged and has remained unchanged for thirty years appears to support the judgment of the Council in reflecting the consensus of the American people.

To protect an aged wife by a monthly allowance while her husband lived, and then to cut her off with a lump-sum settlement on his death, appeared highly illogical, once the concept of adequacy became a paramount consideration. Since women, on average, live longer than men and are usually younger than their husbands, it was clear that payments to aged widows would normally continue for several years after the death of an aged husband. Some part of the cost of these continuing benefits could

139

be recovered by the elimination of the lump-sum return of the balance in the husband's account provided under the 1935 Act. The major cost of the widow's benefit, however, was justified by the new approach to benefits established by the Council: that they should adequately protect the *family unit* and that the mounting income of the system should be used to provide adequate family benefits *soon* rather than to pile up vast reserves for larger individual benefits later.

The Council's recommendations for the protection of surviving widows are succinct and to the point:

> V. The widow of an insured worker, following her attainment of age 65, should receive an annuity bearing a reasonable relationship to the worker's annuity; *provided*, that marital status had existed prior to the husband's attainment of age 60 and one year preceding the death of the husband.

It was stated in the supporting text that an annuity equal to three-fourths of her husband's annuity seemed reasonable. The protection of the widow in her old age was to be based on her husband's record whenever death occurred, except in the case of remarriage.

The new approach did not permit the Council to stop with aged widows. If a younger widow on the death of her husband in mid-life needed protection when she became old, she needed it even more immediately if she had children under her care. The surviving children also needed protection. The Council's recommendation met the problem clearly:

> VI. A dependent child of a currently insured individual upon the latter's death prior to age 65 should

140

receive an orphan's benefit, and a widow of a currently insured individual, provided she has in her care one or more dependent children of the deceased husband, should receive a widow's benefit.

No particular amount of benefit was indicated per child nor was any upper limit on the age of a child proposed. The designations of 50 percent of the primary benefit for each child, subject to a family maximum, and the upper limit of age 18 were made by Congress.

It becomes clear in retrospect, after more than thirty years, that once the Council became convinced that adequate protection of the family unit was the goal of the American social security system, the contingencies to be covered became obvious. The Council agreed on the social desirability of providing benefits for an insured person becoming permanently and totally disabled and to his dependents, but divided on the timing of the introduction of such benefits. Costs and administrative difficulties, and not desirability, were the cause for caution.

The Advisory Council had moved far. It had taken full advantage of the new-found confidence in the mechanism of social insurance which had developed since the Supreme Court had blessed it legally in the previous year and the Treasury had become impressed by the ease of collecting vast sums when benefits were involved.

The recommendations of the Advisory Council of 1937-38 were implemented in the Social Security Act in 1939. The "protection of the family unit" had become so well established as a principle that Congress added a benefit for aged dependent parents should no other eligible dependent survive. Thus, within five years of its conception in 1934 as a plan dealing with contributory old age benefits alone, the revised Social Security Act became the foundation for an integrated social insurance system of family protection.

The arrangements for survivor and dependent benefits under OASDI are still built upon the framework of the 1939 program. The limits of the family unit as an interdependent group have been extended somewhat. The amount of protection, relative to the primary benefit, has been increased for certain categories of dependents, where experience has warranted. In the discussion which follows, the 1939 benefit provisions will be the starting point in summarizing thirty years of change.

Unlike the wife's allowance of 50 percent of the primary benefit, the widow's benefit of 75 percent has undergone considerable change. The wife's allowance is likely to be merged in the mind of the beneficiary into the total payment received. A living husband may still earn supplementary income. But on the husband's death a drop from 150 percent of primary benefit to 75 percent proved an increasing cause of hardship as social conditions changed. The early assumption that aged widows would live with their married children steadily lost validity as millions moved from rural or small-town communities to the impersonal and expensive way of life in a city. The generation gap in terms of neighborhood, friends, child-care, and style of daily living was broadening, and grandmother did not want to make a drastic readjustment after grandfather died. To maintain a separate home for one person costs more than half as much as a household for two, even though the home is owned.

The protection of aged widows became a focus of concern from the mid-1950s on. In 1956, the age of eligibility for a widow's benefit, regardless of children, became 62. In 1961, the basic widow's benefit at 62 was made 82½ percent of her husband's primary benefit. Again, in 1965, it was provided that a widow could begin to draw a survivor's benefit as early as age 60 with an actuarial reduction of 6⅔ percent a year for each year below 62.

The relative amount of protection given the widow under OASDI is still a matter of concern. The change in life patterns of women and the increasing generation gap have greatly reduced any difference in the expectation of continued independence on the part of a widow as compared to a widower or an aged couple. All increasingly prefer to have their own homes. The surveys of benefits received by widows, as well as by single women, confirm the fact, however, that the levels of such benefits are inadequate by almost any standard of comparison. The solution appears clear. The benefit for an aged widow should be 100 percent of her husband's primary benefit. While both husband and wife live, the combined payment would be 150 percent of the primary benefit. When either dies, the survivor would then receive 100 percent of what the husband had received, or two-thirds of the amount for both. There seems to be an understandable logic in such an arrangement which might give it a degree of permanence.

The provision for survivors benefits for younger widows and their children in the 1939 revision of the Social Security Act did more to eliminate the word "orphan" from the American vocabulary than any other development. The realization that the family unit could maintain itself after the death of the father who had been its main support afforded a deep sense of security to the younger adults in the population. Unlike the demand for protection in old age, which had been loudly articulate, the discussion of mothers' and children's allowances had been relatively subdued. The assumption seemed to exist that protection for the young surviving family could come only for those rich enough to have adequate private life insurance or poor enough to be eligible for some form of relief.

The provision for younger survivors in OASDI was very specially the result of intensive self-education of the 1937-38 Advisory Council on Social Security and of the staff of the Social Security Board over many months of study and discussion. During this time, the unique attributes of a compulsory contributory social insurance system compared to private insurance became clear. Since the protection of surviving children involved a definitely limited period from birth to age 18 and, unlike most private life insurance, could be provided by monthly payments precisely fitted to the span of need, the comparative cost was surprisingly moderate. The chances of a father's death increased with his age and so likewise the ages of his surviving children. The termination of children's benefits at 18, as well as the benefit to the young mother when the youngest child became 18, focused protection precisely on the critical period of need. Regular monthly payments, adjusted to family size, were far more effective protection, compared to cost, than large lump sums of insurance arbitrarily selected by the husband years before. The level of protection under social insurance was automatically related to past earnings. Even in the early years, however, the degree of security afforded the young family under OASDI was in striking contrast to that which most wage earners had had previously.

The 1939 Act provided a benefit of 50 percent of the deceased worker's primary benefit for each child, plus 75 percent for the mother. This remained unchanged until 1950, when the benefit for the first child was raised, in effect, to 75 percent with any other children still receiving 50 percent. In 1956, the upper limit of age 18 was eliminated for a child permanently disabled before 18. By 1960, the 75 percent benefit was extended to each child of a deceased worker. The increasing expectation of attending college was reflected in 1965 by a provision that children's benefits could continue from 18 to 21 years of age if the young person was attending school or college. However, the mother's benefit still terminated when the youngest child became 18.

The commendable interest on the part of Congress in providing adequate protection for the family unit of a deceased breadwinner has, from the first, been tempered by the hesitancy of Congress to permit a combination of family benefits to move too far from the previous earnings of the primary beneficiary or to "subsidize" large families. The result has been a repeatedly revised compromise between adequacy and caution, which has produced a series of complicated formulae over the years in the determination of the family maximum benefit in the individual case.

The family maximum set in 1939 was $85, *or* 80 percent of the average monthly wages upon which the primary benefit amount was based, *or* not more than two times the primary benefit amount, whichever was the smaller. The relative liberality of two times the primary

145

benefit amount was thus offset by an arbitrarily set ceiling in dollars and an arbitrarily set relationship to the wages of the deceased averaged over a base period of years. In retrospect, this combination of factors used in setting the family maximum benefit in 1939 was an unfortunate departure from the basic principle of adequacy. It created a precedent of arbitrary adjustment of the family maximum benefit which, at long last, should be corrected.

After seven revisions in over thirty years, the family maximum benefit is still an arbitrary amount without any clearcut justification in terms of adequacy. As of 1970, a family could not receive more than 80 percent of the first $436 of the average monthly wage of the primary beneficiary *plus* 40 percent of the next $214. This arbitrary formula was adjusted in 1971, on the basis of adequacy, to reflect the general cost-of-living increase approved retroactively for that year. The Committee on Ways and Means of the House of Representatives in its report on the 1971 Social Security Amendments speaks of the maximum family benefit as an amount which is a multiple of the primary benefit amount. A uniform multiple does not apply at all benefit levels: the multiples range from 1.5 to 1.88 times the primary benefit amount. At the highest benefit levels the multiple is 1.75 times the primary benefit amount. It is provided, however, again on the basis of adequacy, that the limit cannot be lower, in the individual case, than one and one-half times the primary benefit amount. This means that a widowed mother can receive her benefit of 75 percent of the primary benefit amount and one child an additional 75 percent under the present schedule. The benefits of a three-member family, however, would be reduced to keep them within the maximum limitation applicable to that family.

The long delay in eliminating an arbitrary and inconsistent basis for the determination of the family maximum benefit, and in resolving the issue in terms of the fundamental principle of adequacy, indicates the need for a clearcut philosophy in the development of social security systems. The special limitation upon family benefits related to the previous average wages of the breadwinner seems to have developed out of concepts associated with workmen's compensation insurance. This early form of protection of wage-earners and their families carries with it the unfortunate marks of its evolution. Unlike true social insurance, it reflects a climate of blame, of employer responsibility and differential charges, and of safeguards against employee abuse. Industrial accidents are a distinctly different area of protection from death, by whatever cause, or permanent and total disability, by whatever cause, age included. True social insurance should be primarily based upon imputed need, once a contingency has occurred, not the fear of abuse on the part of the insured, or the desire of a particular employer to control his costs.

Unfortunately, in setting the family maximum the Congress has, in the past, been influenced by the precedents of workmen's compensation in both of the ways indicated. It related the maximum to past average earnings, apart from the general relationship of primary benefits to these earnings, because it was unduly concerned with specific costs or potential abuse. It sought to introduce some notion of "equity," as contrasted to the basic principle of adequacy, in one element in the total pattern of benefits.

147

As an arbitrary invention, the formula became a cost-saving device. The fact that the saving in cost has been at the expense of families in greatest need has proved insufficient to overcome an unfortunate tradition. Perhaps the fear of "subsidizing" large families has also been influential. This should not, however, justify leaving a family with two children with so little protection when the father is deceased.

The principle upon which a family benefit should be based in an internally consistent social insurance system should be the same principle upon which the primary benefit is based, that is, adequacy, subject to an *overall* degree of liberality related to *overall* cost, and to a consistent schedule of graduations reflecting both contribution and incentive. The simplest and most direct way to apply these principles to the family maximum is to make that maximum solely a uniform ratio of the primary benefit amount. The appropriate ratio at this time appears to be two times the primary benefit amount. The reasons for this ratio are several.

The imputed need of the family of a deceased or permanently disabled breadwinner is among the most critical of those which social insurance seeks to meet. Death or disability can occur at any age, and young workers have less chance to save. Further, since the primary benefit is affected by periods of lower early wages, unemployment or illness, it may fall sharply below the recent earnings at the time of death or when disability strikes. Congress has determined that two survivors should receive 150 percent of the primary benefit. To leave three survivors with less than a further 50 percent seems to be

148

an unrealistic discounting of the normal expectancy that an American family will have at least two children.

The imputed need of the family of a permanently disabled beneficiary makes a two-times limit all the more justified. With a primary benefit on behalf of the disabled father, the provision for the wife of 50 percent of this amount and 50 percent more for one child does not seem excessive. Not only may the primary benefit of the disabled person have reflected a growing impairment, but the care of an invalid may be involved.

The arguments for excising the tradition of workmen's compensation insurance from a federal system of social insurance become all the stronger in respect to the present requirement that OASDI benefits must be adjusted where the beneficiaries are also eligible for workmen's compensation payments. The principle of adequacy implemented in the national social insurance program thus gives ground to an inconsistent and questionable tradition inherent in the older state programs. Rather, the national program should stand firm, pay the full OASDI benefit, and let the states adjust their payments as they see fit. The primary beneficiary under OASDI has contributed in order to gain protection for his family as a matter of right. The amount of this protection should not be controlled by the vagaries of state legislation and administration, implementing distinct principles in determining his "compensation" for an industrial accident.

The change from the present arbitrary family maximum amount to a simple ratio of twice the primary benefit would not add greatly either to the adequacy of the protection of the number of families affected or to overall costs. Whatever the cost, however, it would appear to make the social security system more effective in its system of protection and more consistent in its implementation of social insurance principles, and not those of extraneous precedents. To go beyond a two-times ratio at this time appears a questionable step in terms of both balance and the total costs of the system. The aged widow also needs improved protection, and there are other areas of concern in providing adequate security for the American family unit against the wide variety of risks it faces.

# CHAPTER XI

## The Coverage of the Disabled

THE ESSENTIAL LOGIC of protecting workers against the loss of earnings and self-sufficiency because of the onset of permanent and total disability *before* normal retirement became clear to the planners of the American social security program once the possibility of an integrated national system of social insurance became evident. The members of the staff of the Committee on Economic Security assigned to the problem of insecurity in old age were fully aware of the need for such protection and of the fact that foreign social insurance systems covered the risk of permanent disability. But, in 1934, the center of political interest was on the aged, and the risks in attaining any national system of contributory social insurance strongly argued for making protection in old age the primary justification for such a system. The complexities faced in planning for old age benefits were great enough for both the staff and the Congress without adding those involved in disability benefits.

In simplest terms, permanent and total disability is a risk closely parallel to superannuation as a cause of loss of earnings. Both are life risks related to the individual's assumed loss of the physical or mental capacity to continue in gainful employment. Since social insurance benefits are assumed to be a partial replacement of earnings and not a return of savings or a purchased annuity, both old age and disability insurance must utilize tests of eligibility for benefits which take cognizance of the existence or availability of earnings. In the case of old age benefits, once the physical age of eligibility is attained, the earnings-test centers upon the individual's complete or partial withdrawal from covered gainful employment. This, in normal times at least, involves a considerable factor of choice. In the case of disability benefits, however, since the simple determinant of physical age is not applicable, the central emphasis in testing eligibility for benefits becomes the degree of physical or mental impairment of the individual. In a proportion of cases, the medical evidence of total disability may be conclusive, standing alone. In many cases, however, the degree of impairment must be related to a much more difficult form of earnings-test: Has the impairment eliminated, as a supportable determination, the possibility of substantial gainful activity?

It is this necessary relationship between physical or mental condition *and* the possibility of substantial gainful activity which makes the administration of disability insurance so much more difficult than that of old age insurance. It is far easier in a comprehensive contributory social insurance system to check the fact that an aged beneficiary has an amount of earnings than it is to determine that a disabled person cannot work. In old age insurance, the administrator reacts to a choice freely made by the claimant. In disability insurance, he must seek, so far as possible, to obtain objective evidence on conditions beyond the control of the claimant. The absence of earnings is far from sufficient as a test of eligibility. These problems in claims administration, along with financial cost, were major factors in postponing the enactment of a national program for insurance against permanent and total disability until 1956, twenty-one years after the passage of the Social Security Act.

The first indication of official interest in the inclusion of disability insurance under the Social Security Act was the directive to the Advisory Council of 1937-38 that it should consider "the advisability of extending the benefits in Title II to persons who become incapacitated prior to age 65." The Council labored long over the question of whether the newly established social insurance administration could absorb the sticky problems of disability insurance along with the radical changes and additions it was recommending in old age and survivors insurance. The conclusion gave evidence of the arts of creative compromise which made the 1937-38 Council such an effective influence on future legislation:

VII. The provision of benefits to an insured person who becomes permanently and totally disabled and to his dependents is socially desirable. On this point the Council is in unanimous agreement. There is difference of opinion, however, as to the timing of the introduction of these benefits. Some members of the Council favor the immediate inauguration of such benefits. Other members believe that on account of additional costs and administrative difficulties, the problem should receive further study.

The Council was in substantial agreement that the growth of industry and urban life had made the problem of providing for wage earners who became permanently and totally disabled in mid-life increasingly serious. It recognized that the number of the disabled would be small compared to the aged, yet the condition of total disability, when it occurred, created even more serious concerns for the individual, his family, and the commu-

153

nity. Further, it agreed that protection against the hazard, except to the extent that workmen's compensation coverage applied, was even further out of the question for most wage earners than was the protection against dependency in old age.

The members of the Advisory Council who favored immediate inauguration of disability insurance cited the absence of other protection except local relief and the need to avoid pressure for the lowering of the general retirement age. They argued that much of the added cost of disability benefits would replace current expenditures for relief. Insurance benefits would afford a far greater sense of security. Other countries had mastered the administrative problems, and it was suggested that the Social Security Act would never have been passed if it had been postponed until all administrative difficulties had been solved.

The members of the Council opposed to the immediate establishment of disability insurance believed that it would be extremely difficult to estimate costs. It would be better to wait until the costs of old age and survivors insurance became definite before embarking on an additional costly program. They were also deeply concerned about the administrative difficulties, especially in the light of the adverse experience of private companies active in the field. It was believed that, in order to avoid a shifting constituency, disability insurance should await the time when coverage under the system was much broader and administrative experience had been gained.

To meet the argument that private insurance companies had had bad experience in administering disability claims, those favoring early action emphasized the great advantage of a single, compulsory system in checking the earnings of persons claiming or awarded disability benefits. It was difficult to meet the argument of uncertain costs or of the need to develop rapidly a claims system involving medical determinations.

As suggested by the more conservative members of the 1937-38 Council, the problem of coverage of permanent and total disability received continuing study over the next decade culminating in a detailed set of recommendations by the Advisory Council of 1947-48. The need for action had by then become so evident that but two members of the latter Council expressed opposition.

The arguments marshaled by the 1947-48 Council were vigorous and persuasive. It was estimated that two million wage earners were kept from gainful work on a given day by disabilities which had continued for more than six months. The plight of the worker, especially the younger worker with children, was emphasized. The lack of adequate private insurance coverage and the minimal effect of workmen's compensation was noted.

The 1947-48 Advisory Council recommended the extension of coverage to all insured workers, with a strict definition of total and permanent disability and a quadruple test of insured status. To qualify for benefits a disabled person had to be incapable of self-support for an indefinite period because of a condition, demonstrable by objective tests, which would make him unable to perform *any* substantially gainful activity. Even after a waiting period of six months, the disability must appear to be of long-continued and indefinite duration. Eligibility required forty quarters of coverage, one-half of all quarters after 1948, six quarters within the preceding

155

twelve, and two quarters within the preceding four. This was to assure that only currently and regularly employed workers with a long-established participation in the labor market would be eligible. The coverage of the dependents of disabled beneficiaries was not recommended. Thus the Council sought to assure the extension of social insurance to a new risk by restricting eligibility closely and reducing costs to a minimum.

In retrospect, it is difficult to understand the hesitancy of Congress to accept the very limited extension of basic old age and survivors insurance to the new but parallel risk of early disability. A part of that hesitancy arose from the knowledge of the unfavorable experience of private insurance carriers with disability insurance and the failure to recognize the advantages of an almost universal compulsory social insurance system compared to many competing private companies in spreading risks and controlling claims. The Social Security Administration faced no problem of adverse selection of policy holders and had an automatic check on the earnings of persons claiming disability. It did not, however, have the machinery for processing claims based on disablement, since this type of administration was largely confined to the states under workmen's compensation. The idea that a federal insurance agency could use state administrations as agents required time to gain acceptance.

The first break on disability coverage came in 1954, when it was recognized that the hardship imposed upon covered workers who, because of disability, had lost years of earnings in the determination of their old age or survivors protection was both unnecessary and unjustified. The answer was the "disability freeze," introduced in

156

1954, which eliminated, under cautious restrictions, a certified period of total disability in the computation of the average-wage base for other benefits. This required, however, the establishment of machinery to approve claims for such a "freeze," and the ice was broken in entering a new field of administration.

The next steps in the extension of protection against permanent and total disability came rapidly. In 1956, the Congress established disability insurance for covered workers age 50 and over, but not their dependents. In 1958, the dependents of disability beneficiaries were made eligible for benefits. In 1960, the lower age limit of 50 was eliminated. Meanwhile, in 1956, a child disabled before age 18 of a retired or insured deceased worker was covered for benefits after age 18. Disabled children of disabled workers became covered in 1958. The problem of permanent and total disability had, at long last, been recognized. By 1967, the step of protecting disabled widows or dependent widowers over 50 carried forward an evolution from recommendation to legislation which began thirty years before. The process still has a way to go.

The degree of caution reflected in this long evolution of permanent and total disability protection under the American social security system still limits its effectiveness in matching the full impact of long-continued disability as a cause of serious insecurity among American wage earners and their dependents. The gaps which warrant consideration include those arising from the strictness of the initial determination of disability, the definition of the expected continuance of disability, and the length of the waiting period.

157

As discussed earlier in this chapter, permanent and total disability insurance, unlike old age insurance, imposes upon the administrator the often difficult problem of determining that a physical or mental disability prevents the claimant from engaging in any substantial gainful activity. The latter is assumed to include not only his previous occupation but also, considering his age, education, and previous experience, any other kind of substantial gainful work that exists in the national economy. The test disregards the question whether such work exists in the claimant's immediate area, whether a specific job exists, or whether he would be hired if he applied for work. The law reports of the country are replete with court decisions on litigated claims turning on the interpretation of the legislation and regulations covering disability.

Courts and claims administrators will always differ on the precise application of statutory language to cases in which claimants have a large financial stake. The task of the student of social security is to seek the principle which properly balances the needs of the worker for reasonable protection against a cause of hardship beyond his control and the need of a social insurance system to keep costs within reasonable limits.

In developing such a principle in balancing needs, the question arises whether a given physical impairment has the same effect on a young worker and on an older worker in regaining the capacity to earn a living. To learn a new skill or competency usually requires a combination of physical, mental, and psychological aptitudes which must be focused over time on a specific result. In the young, this focusing process comes at a time of flexibility in the choice of occupation and when aptitudes have not become narrowed and reinforced by years of specialization. For the older worker, displaced from his normal employment, the combination of physical, mental, and psychological aptitudes which specialization has reinforced may become an obstacle to change. The change is less difficult if he can return to some skill or capacity learned at an earlier time or which uses a part of the specialized capacities he has gained. The conclusion drawn from practical experience in industry is that, for most workers, a considerable redirection in occupation comes harder after middle age, perhaps 50. This is particularly true when the need for redirection is accompanied by serious decline in physical capacity or endurance.

It is not inconsistent with the assumption that social insurance should protect workers at age 65 who retire because of the aging process that social insurance reflect in disability coverage the effect of aging upon the ability to regain self-sufficiency in a new occupation despite some serious impairment. Rather, it seems reasonable to develop standards of eligibility for disability protection which take age into account. For administrative simplicity, it would be appropriate to establish an age, such as 50, at which the present strict test would be slightly relaxed. A definition of disability at that age might become the inability to engage in substantial gainful activity requiring skills or abilities comparable to those of any gainful activity in which the claimant had been previously engaged with some regularity or over a substantial period of time. The inability to engage in his previous activity or in *any* other kind of substantial gainful work that exists *in the national economy* may be an appropriate requirement for the younger man of 30, but it appears to be too rigid and arbitrary for most workers suffering severe disablement in the last ten or fifteen years of their working life.

It must be remembered that, under a comprehensive social insurance system, the administration still has a check on almost all earnings an older disabled worker might obtain by unusually strenuous efforts on his part. The control of limited, part-time earnings of the older disabled person should have some slight degree of flexibility and be administered with a degree of recognition of the welfare of the beneficiary in total terms and not as merely a device of policing the claims operation. In sum, the balance between adequate protection of the seriously disabled worker and proper control of costs should reflect the actual conditions of life of the disabled. This will require a departure, in some degree, from the tradition of great and persistent caution which has surrounded the evolution of permanent and total disability insurance under the Social Security Act.

The earliest definition of the expected duration of disability to qualify for benefits was that the disability must be expected to result in death or to be of long-continued and indefinite duration. By 1965, long-continued and indefinite duration had been changed to the fact that the disability had lasted or could be expected to last for a continuous period of not less than twelve months. There is increasing reason to believe that the forward estimate of six more months of disability after a six months' waiting period involves both a difficult medical and administrative judgment and, at times, a serious hardship for the claimant. In moving from a position of restrictive caution

160

to a balanced position of matching protection with proven need, as the system matures, it appears desirable to put the emphasis in claim administration on the provable fact that an eligible disability has already existed for six months. The continuing period of protection can be adjusted to the actual events in each case. If a beneficiary recovers the capacity for substantial gainful employment by the ninth or tenth month, benefits can be stopped. The cost to the system is minor. The disabled person, with the loss of six months' earnings during the waiting period, is most certainly in dire need for this limited period of help in overcoming past losses and in regaining self-sufficiency.

The question remains whether a waiting period as long as six months is necessary. Since benefits are paid after the month for which they are due, the first payment for the seventh month is not received by the beneficiary until early in the eighth month. A minimal improvement would be to reduce the waiting period to five months so that payment would reach the beneficiary for the sixth month if he is still disabled, and be available for use during the seventh month. This, at least, would avoid gaps in income if the beneficiary was protected by a company or state plan with the usual maximum duration of benefits of six months.

To reduce the waiting period for a national "permanent and total" disability insurance program below five months involves questions concerning the proper division of responsibility for the protection of disabled persons between the OASDI system and other programs. At one time, it was thought that the states would move into such coverage under temporary disability programs. But only a few states have seen fit to develop such programs. Larger, progressive companies have included temporary disability plans among their fringe benefits. If a national system of health insurance should be developed, it would be logical for that system to cover the first five or six months of medical care with the OASDI system picking up with both family cash benefits and medical care from then on. It is not that we can assume that the burden of both loss of earnings and medical costs should continue to rest upon the worker and his family for a period as long as a half-year, but rather the question of the best way under social insurance we can assist him in meeting this burden. Probably the best answer is the filling of the gap by a national system of health insurance with cash benefits which are coordinated with those under OASDI.

## CHAPTER XII

# The Determination of Individual Benefits

AN IMPORTANT DECISION of the staff of the Committee on Economic Security assigned to old age security in 1934 received little attention at the time but has had fundamental effect on the OASDI system ever since. It was that a system of flat benefits under old age insurance, such as that in Great Britain, was not appropriate for the United States. It was early recognized that a single flat rate of benefits for a country as diversified as the United States would fail to meet the needs of those living in the high-cost urban areas of the North East while being unduly favorable to those in the rural South.

A further reason for avoiding flat benefits was the predisposition of the early planners to carry over to social insurance much of the approach of private annuity plans in relating benefits to past contributions. This was supported by a strong conviction that benefits should reinforce, rather than conflict with, the basic incentives in the American wage system. Since contributions were to be a percentage of wages, and not a flat rate, benefits should bear a relationship to the level of wages earned by the individual, as well as their regularity. The influence of the private annuity approach is shown in an early draft plan of September, 1934, which proposed that the individual beneficiary should receive a basic pension equal to the *actuarial equivalent* of the contributions made to his account *plus* a supplementary pension paid by the Federal Government sufficient to raise the total to a subsistence level. Fortunately, this, like many other early drafts, was soon discarded.

The principle that benefits should be related to each individual's contributions has been a great strength in the support and development of the OASDI program. This is a highly successful carry-over of an American predisposition for rewarding differential effort, as opposed to the assumption in older, class-oriented societies that social insurance for workers need only provide a common level of protection.

The staff planners in the Committee on Economic Security failed to go the full way in visualizing a class-free program, however. In the early drafts and in the recommendations to Congress, an upper limit was set on the level of earnings received by an individual to bring him under coverage. In the earliest draft, all manual workers were to be covered and non-manual workers to a maximum of $250 a month. The recommendation of a monthly wage limit on coverage of *individuals* was, fortunately, eliminated by the Congress. Thus *all* persons earning income through gainful employment in the covered industries and occupations were made subject to compulsory contributions up to a ceiling of covered *earnings* and therefore became eligible for benefits. The American system of social security was, therefore, established on a basis that ignored class levels.

It was assumed from the first that the relation of benefits to past wages should not be constant at all levels, but, rather, that the scale of benefits should be graduated in a manner to favor the lower-paid worker. It was considered sound social insurance philosophy, as opposed to that of private insurance, to give clear emphasis to adequacy as balanced against equity in paying higher proportional benefits where these were needed to provide the bare essentials of living, tapering off as benefits rose above this level. This philosophy has apparently reflected the predispositions of the American people, since it has seldom, if ever, been challenged.

The first crude implementation of the principle of graduated benefits appeared in the 1935 Act. In the haste to find a formula and the need to avoid more than minimal connection between contributions and benefits because of constitutional hazards, individual benefits were based on *cumulative* wage credits during the covered worker's lifetime. The benefit formula included three steps: ½ percent of the first $3,000 of cumulated wage credits; $\frac{1}{12}$ percent of the next $42,000; and $\frac{1}{24}$ percent of the next $84,000. Under this formula, a worker earning a total of $3,000 over a span of time as short as one year or more could receive $15 a month. A worker receiving $45,000 over at least fifteen years, since the maximum of covered wages was $3,000, would receive a benefit of $50 a month. The highest benefit possible was $85 a month, which could only be attained in a lifetime of earnings of $3,000 a year for 43 years. To indicate the effect of the graduations, three beneficiaries, all employed twenty-five years at $1,000, $2,000, and $3,000 a year, respectively, would receive at 65, $33.33, $52.08, and $62.50 a month. Thus, three times the level of wages was designed to produce well under twice the benefit.

Fortunately, this formula for benefits never went into effect, since well before first benefits were to be paid in 1942, the drastically changed approach recommended by the Advisory Council of 1937-38 was implemented in the

Act of 1939. Not only would the original formula have delayed adequate benefits for many, many years, but it would have failed to recognize the effect of even a very modest contribution rate in producing income sufficient to pay much higher benefits in the early years. The cumulative wage factor and the graduated scale, together, would have produced arbitrary results in individual benefits which would depart greatly from the particular needs of the individual, especially in the early years.

The Advisory Council, with adequate time for study, recognized that the best basis for determining benefits was to relate them to the *average* of the wages earned and which needed to be replaced in some graduated degree when retirement occurred. The effectiveness of the payroll tax in accumulating funds, and the common desire to avoid further delay in getting adequate benefits to the elderly, made the average-wage concept attractive to both the Council and the Congress. The use of the average wage brought the system out of the long future to the present in attacking the problem of insecurity. It also was the first step in the evolution of understanding that a national contributory social insurance program involved essentially a current redistribution of cash flows and not a partial compromise between *private* reserve insurance and truly *social* insurance.

The shift to the average-wage base was one of the most important contributions of the Advisory Council of 1937-38. While refinements in the years covered in the average came later, the earliest implementation in the Act of 1939 used the simple approach of average covered wages to retirement in the period since 1936, excluding calendar quarters in which less than $50 was earned before age 22.

The graduation in individual benefits was implemented by a formula of 40 percent of the first $50 of average monthly wage *plus* 10 percent of the next $200. The highly cautious figure of $40 at the maximum was to be increased by a factor of 1 percent of the amount thus determined for each year in which the beneficiary had earned at least $200. Even after 25 years, the maximum benefit payable would be but $50. In 1939, the purchasing power of the dollar was still undiminished by inflation. The Congress was still very conservative in its estimate of what payroll taxes could produce or in judging what the American people were willing to pay for old age and survivors insurance.

By 1950, with many old people on benefit, a steady upward movement of benefit levels began. Congress had begun to learn that there was widespread interest in benefit levels. On the advice of the Advisory Council of 1947-48, the Congress eliminated the last vestige of the old concept of a time-related cumulative factor in the benefit scale. The increment of 1 percent for each year of covered earnings was recognized as merely a postponement of adequate benefits, as well as an unfortunate complication in the forward financing of the system. The new formula became 50 percent of the first $100 and 15 percent of the next $200, sufficient to provide a maximum of $80 a month. In 1954, this was changed to 55 percent of the first $110 and 20 percent of the next $240, with a maximum of $108.50. From then on, the formula has been revised repeatedly to implement general benefit increases and to adjust the estimated costs of new scales to actuarial requirements. In 1958, the percentage formula was replaced in large part by a table of benefits set forth in the

167

law. The table, in turn, was based on percentages related to segments of average earnings combined and rounded out in a series of small intervals.

In the seventeen years from 1954 to 1971, the benefit structure under OASDI had come a long way. For comparison, the benefits payable for given average earnings are shown below:

| Average Monthly Earnings | Benefit Scale in 1954 Revision | Benefit as a Percentage of AME (1954) | Benefit in Effect in 1971 | Benefit as a Percentage of AME (1971) | Percentage Rise in Benefits from 1954 to 1971 |
|---|---|---|---|---|---|
| $ 76 | $ 41.80 | 55.0 | $ 70.40 | 92.6 | 68.4 |
| 110 | 60.50 | 55.0 | 99.70 | 90.6 | 64.8 |
| 150 | 68.50 | 45.7 | 111.90 | 74.6 | 63.4 |
| 200 | 78.50 | 39.3 | 128.60 | 64.3 | 63.8 |
| 250 | 88.50 | 35.4 | 145.60 | 58.2 | 64.5 |
| 350 | 108.50 | 31.0 | 177.70 | 50.8 | 63.8 |
| 450 | .... | .... | 208.80 | 46.4 | .... |
| 550 | .... | .... | 240.30 | 43.7 | .... |
| 650 | .... | .... | 275.80 | 42.4 | .... |
| 750 | .... | .... | 295.40 | 39.4 | .... |

The improvement in the total scale of benefits has been most impressive. The proportion of average monthly earnings replaced has been greatly improved. The degree of improvement has, however, been uniform in percentage terms for all earnings above an average of $100 a month because of the across-the-board approach implemented by Congress in reflecting cost-of-living changes. Since the bend-point in the slope of the graduations in relating benefits to average earnings was set at $110 a month in 1954, no further change in the bend-point has been made. Rather, the new slope of graduations has been the old slope lifted at each point by a constant percentage improvement on the assumption that the rise in the cost of living affects all beneficiaries in the same proportion.

From the point of view of Congress, the upward adjustment of the benefit scale by a constant percentage has considerable political advantage. It can be announced that all benefits are raised by a given percent. Such an announcement has the advantage of simplicity and also helps quiet objection to any accompanying rise in the ceiling on covered wages. If those paying higher contributions in the upper range of earnings were not to receive the standard cost-of-living adjustment, they might feel aggrieved.

From the point of view of social insurance policy, however, there is real question whether the lifting of a benefit scale by a constant percentage throughout the scale is appropriate. Graduations in social insurance benefit scales are intended to provide a greater replacement of the lost earnings for lower-paid workers than for higher-paid workers. This is because the lower-paid worker as a beneficiary *must* use a much higher proportion of his benefit on essential expenditures such as food, clothing, and housing. With inflation, the lower-income beneficiary cannot avoid paying the higher prices for these essentials, and there is strong reason, therefore, to believe that a higher proportion of his income must be assigned to them. The higher-income beneficiary is also affected, but has a larger margin of remaining income to draw upon. For these reasons, it appears proper, when inflation occurs, to shift the scale of benefits upward at the lower end of scale for those who can barely live on their insurance benefits without supplementary public assistance to a somewhat greater degree than for those at the higher end

169

of the scale. This can be done by revising the table of benefits to introduce a more favorable ratio of benefits to average wages in the lower levels of the scale than the ratio in the present scale *without* carrying fully this more favorable ratio up through the higher levels. The advantage of the table of benefits now used is that the method of building the scale by accumulated percentages of segments of average earnings, still carried over as the basis for the table, can be discarded so that the structure of the table can reflect any pattern desired.

The appropriate zone in which a more favorable ratio of benefits to average wages should be introduced in a time of rising costs of living is that which centers about the benefits received by *regularly employed* lower-wage workers. This zone starts well above the minimum benefit level since many beneficiaries at the lowest end of the scale are there because of limited employment under OASDI coverage. This may have been the result of regular employment in the federal or other governmental services, limited dependence on earnings, such as with married women, or casual employment of some kind. Since many of these beneficiaries will have other sources of protection, including public assistance, it does not seem appropriate for the scale of benefits under a contributory social insurance system to be patterned to match their specific needs. Rather, the present benefit scale under OASDI is already favorable to the person of limited, intermittent coverage. It is the worker who has worked and contributed regularly throughout life, but at a lower level of wages, who should receive favorable treatment in the benefit scale in a time of rising costs, so that he or his dependents will not need to resort to public assistance to supplement an inadequate insurance benefit when earnings cease.

The foregoing discussion of benefit scales raises again the basic concept of adequacy which must underlie social insurance policy as compared to that appropriate for private insurance programs. The graduated scale under social insurance implements a policy of social redistribution of income in order to assure adequate protection. For the present, under OASDI, this redistribution is that of a flow of funds derived from payroll taxes, with certain minor exceptions. If, in the future, it is necessary to adjust the pattern of the benefit scale to provide relatively more adequate protection at the lower levels, and there is objection to this increased degree of social distribution of funds derived from payroll taxes, the need to introduce a government contribution derived from general taxes may become evident. The choice of Congress thus far is to avoid the question of a government contribution by keeping benefits at the upper end of the scale attractive at the expense of meeting the greater relative needs of the regularly-employed lower-wage worker. The device has been across-the-board percentage increases throughout the whole scale. With the rise in the level of assistance payments, especially should public assistance become nationalized, the inadequacy of OASDI benefits at the lower levels in the scale will become clear. Should inflation continue, the problem will become acute. The problem of assuring adequate benefits at the lower levels of the OASDI scale will not be made easier should the Congress make drastic increases in the ceiling on taxable covered earnings.

The fact that there has not been serious objection to

171

increases in the ceiling on covered wages in the past is little assurance that such objection may not develop if adjustments proceed faster than average earnings throughout the country. During the period of development of OASDI, new categories of protection have been added, benefits have been liberalized, and there has been a general anticipation of better things to come. Meanwhile, incomes have risen steadily, especially in organized industries and services. But as the pattern of OASDI matures, other deductions from earnings develop, general taxes increase, and if the rate of increase in earnings slows down, the relative attractiveness of OASDI protection to its cost for the higher-paid worker may decline. It is then that those near the ceiling of coverage, who have contributed without benefit for many years, may question the degree of social redistribution in the OASDI system.

In the change to the use of average wages in the computation of benefits, implemented in the legislation of 1939, it was assumed that the average would be determined by the simple method of dividing the individual's total covered earnings by the number of years from 1937 when contributions began (or age 22) to the time of retirement or death. When coverage was broadly expanded in 1950, the alternative starting date of 1951 was established, not only for persons newly covered, but for all who would be benefited thereby. In 1954, when additional groups were covered, instead of establishing a new starting date, provision was made for dropping out the four years of lowest earnings in the computation of the average. By 1956, a drop-out of 5 years, available for persons of longer coverage in the 1954 Act, was made universal.

In addition to the earlier changes in the starting point and dropping out low years, the base period for averaging earnings was limited, in 1960, to the year in which the worker reached normal retirement age—62 for women, 65 for men. Where covered individuals continue to work beyond normal retirement age, it was established that the number of years in the base period for computation purposes would not be increased beyond the number applicable at retirement age. This meant that, in addition to the normal drop-out of the 5 years of lowest earnings from his computation period, a male worker having years of earnings *after* attainment of age 65 that were better than any of those remaining in his computation period (after the drop-out) would have these better years used in determining his average earnings for benefit purposes. This afforded a considerable advantage to persons continuing full-time work reaching retirement age since not only additional years of low earnings would be excluded, but also, for higher-paid workers, the years when the ceiling on covered earnings were lower than in more recent years.

An illustration of the procedure might be helpful, even though explained earlier, since this element in benefit computation is often overlooked. A male worker becoming 65 in 1971 has completed 20 full years of coverage under OASDI coverage, the years 1951 to 1970 inclusive. His computation base becomes, because of the 5-year drop-out, his best 15 years of earnings. If he ceases to earn at this point, his benefit will continue to be determined on this basis. If, however, he works sufficiently in 1971 to have earnings better than in any of the years from 1951 to 1970, after his five worst years have been eliminated, the earnings of 1971 will be substituted for the remaining worst year. If he has worked at the covered maximum throughout the whole period, the result can be readily shown. In the 20-year period from 1951 to 1970, the ceiling on covered earnings rose from $3,600 to $7,800. A 5-year drop-out would eliminate 4 years at $3,600 and one year at $4,200. By earning $7,800 in 1971, he will add a $7,800-year in substitution of a $4,200-year. His average yearly earnings will then be raised by $\frac{1}{15}$ of the difference between $4,200 and $7,800 (i.e., $3,600), or $240; his average monthly earnings by $\frac{1}{12}$ of $240, or $20.

The recomputation of benefits for persons working after the normal time of retirement will, of course, improve benefits only for those whose covered earnings during a year are better than in one or more of the years previously used in their computation base. With the steady rise in wages in recent years and the repeated lifting of the ceiling on covered earnings, however, this element in benefit determination should have some slight effect in recognizing the continuing productivity of older persons. It may, to some extent, soften the impact of the continuing contributions required.

In the case of women, the terminal point of the base period was reduced to age 62 in 1961, while that for men continued to be age 65. It was assumed that women retired from regular gainful employment earlier than men and that the inclusion of the 3 years of low or no earnings

174

from 62 to 65 would excessively reduce average earnings and, therefore, benefits.

With the increasing number of men claiming benefits before 65 in recent years because of partial disability, unemployment, or less serious reasons, pressure has developed to reduce the terminal point in the averaging period to age 62 for them as well. As discussed earlier, there are questions concerning the advisability of such a change. If it should encourage the general establishment of age 62 as the customary age of retirement for men, it would have widespread economic and cultural repercussions. If it is considered merely as a means of improving the benefits for persons permanently displaced from employment in later life for reasons beyond their control, it has some justification, especially in the absence of adequate protection against the special hazards faced by partially disabled, older workers in regaining normal employment once displaced. It is true that retirement before age 65 would still involve an actuarial reduction in the benefit paid for the remainder of the beneficiary's life. This very obvious cost of early retirement would be likely to have far more effect on an individual's decision than a one-time change in the method of computing average wages.

A lowering of the terminal point from 65 to 62 for men, if applied to all current male beneficiaries, would add another 3 years of drop-out to the 5 already provided. This one-time change would improve average earnings for a great many beneficiaries. Benefits would be improved for all persons whose covered earnings had risen during the period from 1951 until retirement, for those who had long periods of low or uncovered earnings, and for those whose covered earnings were limited by the earlier lower ceilings. The cost would be very considerable. If the change in the terminal point from 65 to 62 were applied only to new beneficiaries in the future, the cost would be much less. Many men now on benefit would not obtain the advantage of the improvement in their average earnings involved in an across-the-board change.

An issue remains whether any further dropping-out of years of low earnings would be justified as the normal years of coverage under OASDI increase. For a man retiring at age 65 in 1971, the base period used is 20 years (starting with 1951) less 5 years, or 15 years. If the terminal point was changed to age 62, this would reduce the computation base period to his best *12* years out of the 20. This appears to be a liberal arrangement. However, if a man retires in 1994 at age 65, he will have worked 43 years since 1951. A drop-out of 8 years in 43 may then seem insufficient to offset periods of unusually low earnings. There appears to be no reason, however, to press for any further change in the base period in the near future if the terminal point is reduced to age 62. It is questionable whether there will ever be reason, under the present system, to drop out more than a quarter of the normal number of years of employment from age 22 to age 65. This would eventually limit the drop-out to 10 or 11 years compared to 8, if a 62-year terminal point was introduced.

The method of dropping out a number of years from a worker's record in computing OASDI benefits is primarily justified as a means of adjusting a benefit to his *individual* imputed need. It is an attempt to base benefits on the individual worker's *normal* level of earnings, un-affected by periods of no earnings or low earnings caused by shorter intermittent spells of illness, disability, unem-ployment, continuing education, or employment in non-covered activities. It is not intended to produce normal benefits for those who have, during a large part of their adult life, been engaged in non-covered employment under federal or other governmental benefit programs. Nor is it expected to offset long periods during which a housewife has withdrawn from the labor market. The drop-out method is peculiarly a social insurance device to adjust benefits to a pattern of need as related to the *normal* covered earnings of the individual. It is not, pri-marily, a method of reflecting changes in the general cost of living.

Under OASDI, general increases in the cost of living can be offset by raising the whole scale of benefits from time to time. This is possible under compulsory contribu-tory social insurance since the income of the system can be increased by both contribution rate increases and by lifting the ceiling on covered earnings. If dollars become cheaper because of inflation, both income and outgo can be adjusted to the cheaper dollars. Financed largely on a current-transfer basis, social insurance does not have the problem of private reserve insurance where both pre-miums and benefits are normally determined in fixed dollars. Also, under private annuity programs, the use of a lifetime average of earnings as a basis for benefits seri-ously reduces the benefit paid. Such programs have sought to offset this effect by basing retirement annuities on an average of earning over a much shorter period, the last ten years of earnings, for example. Because of the freedom to adjust the whole scale, such a device is unnecessary under social insurance as implemented under OASDI.

To base OASDI benefits on the last or highest five or ten years of covered earnings, as sometimes proposed, overlooks this difference between social and private insurance programs. To shift to such a limited computation base, and still retain the present method of adjusting to cost of living, would be extremely costly. Under social insurance, cost-of-living adjustments need to be made for beneficiaries long on the rolls regardless of their earnings records. The introduction of a five- or ten-year computation base would, for a time, help new beneficiaries coming on the rolls, but this advantage might be lost in a few years of continuing inflation. It seems wise policy, therefore, to determine *individual differences* in benefits through the use of life earnings with drop-out years sufficient to assure a normal individual level, and then to adjust the whole scale for all beneficiaries from time to time for *general factors* affecting all, such as a rising cost of living.

## CHAPTER XIII

# The General Problems of
# Financing the OASDI Program

SOCIAL SECURITY IN THE UNITED STATES, as implemented by the Social Security Act of 1935, had its
genesis in the midst of a vigorous debate on how a contributory social insurance system should be financed. The
question was not whether payroll taxes on employers and
employees should provide the funds, at least for some
time to come, but rather how to balance income and
outgo over the long future. A great national compulsory
system of insurance was such a novel concept that many
leaders in government were unable to grasp the fundamental difference between it and a vast enlargement of
private annuity insurance.

The Cabinet Committee on Economic Security was
split on the issue of long-run financing. The Secretary of
the Treasury, Henry Morgenthau, insisted that a large
reserve be accumulated to help meet future drains. The
old age staff of the Committee was firmly opposed, but
the Secretary won his point with President Roosevelt. As
originally enacted, the old age insurance system would
have accumulated in time a reserve of $47 billion, more
than the outstanding debt of the government in 1935.

The position of those favoring a large reserve was a
clear reflection of the proper policies of a *private* insurance company. Since wage credits under the system would
involve increasingly heavy out-payments in the years
ahead, this accruing liability should, they argued, be bal-

anced by a growing reserve sufficient, along with interest and then current income, to meet this liability when due. The exponents of this policy never went the full way. They avoided consideration of the sticky problems of economic deflation while the vast reserve was building or that of just how it could be invested without absorbing most of the outstanding federal debt.

The nub of the problem in the issue of the large reserve was the stretch of mind required to see that, under a government system of compulsory social insurance, the financial obligations incurred were of such dimensions that only the taxing power of the government could be the essential security for their fulfillment. The securities of the government for the government itself are but an evidence of obligation. To a private individual or a private insurance company, they are prime assets. To the government, they were merely an advanced assignment of funds which must eventually be raised by taxes.

It is easy for an economist to be critical of the general public for not undergoing the mind-stretching operation of putting reserves under a national compulsory insurance system into broad perspective. The symbol of reserves in government bonds runs all through our economic system, in banks, insurance companies, endowments, reserve funds, and private savings. Even the states and cities of the country invest their reserves in them. That the symbol should change its character when the United States government, the issuer, uses them as reserves, takes some degree of analysis. Confusion is increased if the person who argues that the government should hold large reserves in government bonds against future insurance payments simultaneously complains that

180

the proceeds of the sale of government bonds are used to buy battleships or to balance deficits.

Gradually, over the decades since 1935, a general faith in the government's commitment to make good on its social insurance obligations, through assuring sufficient income in the system, has diluted the early anxiety concerning the size of reserves. The present reserves of the system, which are in the general dimension of one year's obligations, are a very small factor in assuring security, even though thirty or more billion dollars looks big to the ordinary citizen. The shift in attitude has not come so much through economic analysis as through the pragmatic conclusion that the mechanism of financing, thanks to the Social Security Administration and the House Ways and Means Committee, seems to work. The social security system as a whole has sold itself. The common reaction is: Why look under the hood?

To the economist, the financing of the OASDI system is but a special case of current redistribution of flows of national income which takes place in many aspects of governmental operations. The old are taxed to educate the young, the city-dwellers are taxed to subsidize the farmers, and the rich are taxed to support the destitute. The particular distinguishing element in contributory social insurance is that the payment of a tax establishes certain individual rights to future benefits. Most of the funds, however, in the immediate plane of time, are redistributed with little if any delay.

Old age insurance does, however, have the special characteristic of transferring funds between generations—those working and those retired. This, however, is not too far different from the age old custom of a son supporting his parents in their later life. Disability and survivor benefits constitute transfers, in many cases, within a generation. Health insurance, covering medical costs, may constitute a form of current transfer among a single age group.

Social insurance policy has long implemented another principle of redistribution which distinguishes it from private insurance, but not from the general policies of government. This is, as has been discussed repeatedly, the application of the concept of adequacy in providing a higher relative replacement of lost earnings to those with the greatest imputed need. The use of graduated benefits under social insurance is but a special case of *social* redistribution which goes on throughout a community or nation.

While the general concept of current redistribution of funds may provide a basis for the financial policy of a vast compulsory social insurance system, how does one make it work? To balance varying income flows with varying outgo flows, year by year, one must return to the concept of reserves, but for a distinctly different purpose. Just as a city water system needs on-line reservoirs to equalize flows, so a social insurance system needs an equalizing reserve. In times of depression, payroll taxes may provide a reduced flow, but the old, the disabled and the surviving families need undiminished benefits. More people may retire early at such a time. There is need, therefore, for a *contingency* or *equalization* reserve to avoid the necessity of sudden changes in contribution rates.

Evolving experience has come to justify a reserve fund under OASDI of approximately one year's benefits. To

182

build up more involves a withdrawal of funds from public consumption which might prove deflationary for the general economy and distort the fiscal program of the government. To build up less might prove unfortunate if, during a long depression, benefits might exceed income for several years. In this case, the reserves would need to be drawn upon to supplement, by a minor proportion, the ongoing income from the great majority of the people who continue to contribute. In addition to equalizing varying flows caused by economic conditions, the reserve helps to offset any miscalculations in actuarial estimates, such as trends in longevity, the age of retirement, mortality during working life, or the incidence of disability. In a nationwide program, such actuarial factors can be estimated closely, but there is still need for the cushion of a contingency reserve.

It is easier to decide that a reserve of one year's obligation is appropriate than to make sure that the net differential of inflows and outflows adds just enough to reserves to come out to the proper figure. Rates of contribution are changed periodically by congressional action. A small increase in rate or a change in the ceiling on coverage may increase income faster than expected, especially if earnings are rising throughout the country. For example, the reserve for old age and survivors insurance rose from $28.2 billion to $32.6 billion from the end of fiscal year 1969 to the end of fiscal year 1970. Cash benefits in the latter year were $26.3 billion. During the first ten months of 1970, the reserve varied from $29.8 billion to $32.1 billion. The separate reserve for disability insurance in June, 1970, was $5.1 billion, whereas cash benefit payments were $2.8 billion during the fiscal year then closing. Since changes in business conditions and variations in benefit payments, as affected by both economic and legislative changes, are bound to alter the net income of the system, it is probable that a reserve varying within the limits of 75 percent to 125 percent of annual outgo is a reasonable application of the guide line of approximating one year's benefit.

The task of estimating the income and outgo of the OASDI system so as to assure a net balance year by year, plus a proper reserve, requires the continuous efforts of a staff of actuaries and economists. Not only must estimates be as accurate as possible for the years immediately ahead, but the long-run costs well into the next century must be analyzed to prevent commitments to persons now young from exceeding in total volume a reasonable charge upon the contributors of the future. It has been the practice over the years for Congress to establish in the Social Security Act, as amended, a schedule of contribution rates for the indefinite future which would afford actuarial balance with the expected cost of benefits and administration. While carefully estimated, these rates have been set aside whenever actuarial estimates for the years immediately ahead showed them to involve a departure from accepted guidelines in respect to the size of the reserves. This dichotomy between the legislative implementation of long-run estimates to assure *eventual* balance and the practical application of shorter-run estimates to assure *current* balance has been a continuing issue in the actuarial planning of the OASDI system. Fortunately, time has always permitted a shift from legally established rates to rates adapted to current needs before any serious distortion in reserve policy has occurred.

The practice of implementing long-run actuarial estimates of necessary contributions in the law and then changing them when they prove unnecessary may seem somewhat irrational if taken out of the context of American social insurance experience. It grows out of the constant desire of the Congress, and particularly of the Ways and Means Committee of the House, to assure the American people of the "actuarial soundness" of the system. While the American people have come to realize that the OASDI system, unlike private insurance programs, does not require a "full actuarial reserve," they still seem to feel, or at least Congress believes that they feel, more assured of the "actuarial soundness" of the system if it can be shown that income and outgo will balance over many decades ahead. It is true, also, that such a concept of long-run balance is an effective restraint upon excessive liberality in benefits. Each time an improvement in benefit rates or coverage is introduced, a balancing addition to the contribution rates in the long-run schedule has been established in the law. Even though these precise rates may never become effective, they are believed to have served a purpose assuring the people of the security of the program and the cautious self-restraint of Congress.

The actuarial history of the OASDI system has been one of moving from a long-run theoretical actuarial balance in financing to a pragmatic application of shorter-run actuarial analysis. Not only has the program undergone constant adjustment in the level and scope of benefits, but the ability and willingness of the American people to pay higher contributions on a higher segment of earnings in order to pay for those benefits has under-

185

gone constant change upward. It is most difficult to estimate the conditions influencing income and outgo in
perpetuity or even in the year 2020. The eventual contribution rates established in the legislation have become
more and more theoretical at the same time that the
OASDI system has become more and more established
as a vital mechanism in the lives of the people.

This shift in emphasis from long-run to shorter-run
actuarial estimates has been apparent in the recommendations of succeeding Advisory Councils. The demand
placed upon the actuarial staff of the OASDI administration, however, has not become less but greater.
Shorter-run estimates involve an extension of a host of
economic, social, demographic, administrative, and political factors from past experience into a future which is
near enough for them to be more precisely relevant. No
longer can estimates serve which assume constant levels
of wages and benefits and leave variations to be compensated later. Based upon a philosophy of current-cost
financing, the financial planning of the system has become more and more an implementation of this philosophy. Actuarial soundness is becoming a term more truly
applicable to a vast compulsory contributory social insurance system and less a vague carryover from private insurance or private bookkeeping.

The increased emphasis upon shorter-run actuarial estimates in OASDI financing suggests that the time has
come to avoid statutory enactment of a presumptive
schedule of contribution rates for long years ahead. This
does not imply, however, that the Social Security Administration and the Congress can avoid the preparation and
analysis of long-run factors of cost in their consideration

186

of any changes in the financing and benefit structure of the system. Any change in benefit scale or coverage does affect the cost of the system in perpetuity. Its cost, relative to the ongoing costs of the present system, must be estimated. This can be stated in terms of the percentage of payroll required to finance it. Only by such comparisons can the relative advantage of one changeover against another be evaluated in terms of the effectiveness of the total social security program. The sum of the additional costs arising from changes in benefit structure must be weighed against the best short-run and long-run estimates of income in order to determine whether they can be reasonably financed over time.

Should benefits and ceilings on covered earnings become automatically related to cost of living and average earnings, statutory schedules of contribution rates carried into the long future would become all the more hypothetical. The continuing need for long-run estimates will be to provide the best possible aides to *judgment* of how fast and how far the social security system should be expanded, rather than to give an impression of "actuarial soundness" by formally announcing precise contribution schedules many years ahead. Long-run estimates of cost have always been educated judgments and not precise controls. The newer approach in OASDI financial planning has come to recognize this fact.

It has been the assumption in Congress for many years that the OASDI system will continue to be financed by payroll taxes alone. This has added to the importance of accurate forward estimates of cost, since the willingness of American workers and their employers to pay a given level of tax is by no means a foregone conclusion. Even though retirement annuities are now an established part of the fringe benefit programs of larger employers, the segment provided by OASDI can become too costly. The employee and, especially, the self-employed are bound to weigh their tax payments against the protection gained. This will be increasingly true as contributions increase. In the absence of any contribution by government to the basic OASDI system, the planners of the system must, therefore, design a careful course in a time of mounting current costs in balancing the level of the protection desired by the people concerned and their willingness, year by year, to meet the cost of that protection through payroll taxes. This will be, essentially, a political judgment, but it will necessarily be based on accurate estimates of that cost.

The original planners of the system assumed that the government would eventually share in the cost of the program. It is interesting to note that the old age staff of the Committee on Economic Security proposed that when the reserve fell below a predetermined level, the government should contribute a sufficient flow of funds to maintain that level. Under such an arrangement, the present planners of the system would have a cushion for error which they do not have today. To assure actuarial soundness in its proper sense, there is now no substitute for the highest order of judgment in both the Administration and Congress.

There remains the question of how the contingency or equalization reserves of the OASDI system should be invested. In some foreign social insurance schemes, reserves have been invested in various public projects such as housing or hospitals. It has always been the policy in

American programs to invest reserves in the general securities of the national government and to avoid any involvement in how the government uses the proceeds. The ideal has been to have the financing of OASDI as neutral as possible in its effect on general fiscal operations. A large part of reserve funds are invested in special issues designed for this purpose alone, rather than in public issues. The great dimensions of the federal debt and of current fiscal operations have been an advantage in retaining such a neutral posture.

It has been strongly urged by succeeding Advisory Councils that this posture of neutrality be maintained despite the growth of social insurance income and disbursements. The repeated recommendation that the size of the reserve be kept as close as possible to one year's benefit payments is based, in large part, on this concept of neutrality. Pronounced changes in social security reserves through unwise planning of contribution schedules or benefit disbursements were to be avoided to limit any inflationary or deflationary effects on the general economy. Advisory Councils have likewise urged that the fiscal agencies of the government avoid any tendency to interfere in the determination of social security policy for the ulterior purpose of easing their current fiscal problems. This trade-off of neutrality on the part of two major agencies of government which deal with large flows of funds in respect to each other's policies is of great importance in maintaining the integrity of the American social insurance system. If the system became an instrument of fiscal policy, the precious confidence of the American people would be undermined. The system in its own normal operations provides a stabilizing factor in the American

189

economy. But its primary purpose is to provide security to the individual American worker and his family. It should not be distorted into a mechanism for the manipulation of fiscal balances.

Since the major proportion of the reserves for the OASDI system is invested in special issues, there is the question of the rate of interest which should be set on these issues. Again, repeated Advisory Councils have studied the question. The conclusion has been that the return on social security reserves should approximate as closely as possible the cost of funds to the government as determined by the yields on federal securities issued for an intermediate span of years. In the earlier years, it was found that neither the *coupon* rates on securities of longer span nor the *yield* rate on such securities provided the social security system with a precisely proper return. Bonds with due dates fifteen years ahead might continue a coupon rate of return well below current yields, if interest rates were rising. The best test of the cost of money which the OASDI system automatically makes available to the Treasury appears to be the *yield* which the Treasury must afford to other lenders to furnish money for a four- to seven-year period. Since any major fluctuation in OASDI reserves is likely to be within this time dimension, and since a large part of the reserves will never be withdrawn, the yield rate on government securities of this duration seems reasonable to all concerned. Again, the effort has been to find a position of neutrality in assuring that neither the Treasury nor the social security system gains any advantage in the investment of social security reserves over against the best possible measurement of the true cost of funds otherwise obtained.

At the time the original Social Security Act was drafted in 1935 it was felt necessary for constitutional reasons to separate legally the taxation and benefit features of the program. With the decisions of the Supreme Court in 1937, this separation was no longer necessary. The Advisory Council of 1937-38 recommended that the taxes levied as contributions to the old age insurance program be automatically credited to an old age insurance fund. It was believed that such a procedure would enhance public understanding of the contributory insurance system. Its recommendation was precise as to the nature of the fund.

> The old-age insurance fund should specifically be made a trust fund, with designated trustees acting on behalf of the prospective beneficiaries of the program. The trust fund should be dedicated exclusively to the payment of the benefits provided under the program and, in limited part, to the costs necessary to the administration of the program.

The Council also recommended that the old age insurance fund should continue to be invested in the securities of the federal government, as had been the practice from the first.

In accord with the Council's recommendation, the Congress, in 1939, established a board of trustees for the old age insurance fund consisting of the Secretary of the Treasury, as chairman and managing trustee, the Secretary of Labor, and the Chairman of the Social Security Board. After the Department of Health, Education and Welfare was established, the secretary of that department replaced the chairman of the Social Security Board. The

191

commissioner in charge of the Social Security program became the secretary of the board. The board makes reports to the Congress each year, but appears to depend entirely upon the actuarial and financial officers of the Social Security Administration and the Treasury in their preparation, rather than having any staff of its own. The annual meetings of the board are said to be perfunctory.

Experience over the years indicates that the common board of trustees of the now separate reserve funds for old age insurance, disability, hospital, and medical insurance should become more than a vehicle for passing on reports to Congress. There is no question but that the Social Security Administration and the Treasury have shown the highest order of responsibility in the safeguarding and management of social security funds. But the recommendation of the Advisory Council of 1937-38 called for trustees "acting on behalf of the prospective beneficiaries of the program." Further, the three last Advisory Councils have raised questions about the rate of return on social security funds as affected by the policies and procedures followed by the Treasury. Changes have been made because of Advisory Council recommendations which might properly have been initiated sooner by the board of trustees, if it had acted "on behalf of the beneficiaries of the program." Rather, the board has allowed the staffs of the Social Security Administration and the Treasury to work out a balance of mutual accommodation. The Secretary of the Treasury, as managing trustee, and the Secretary of Health, Education and Welfare, as a fellow cabinet member, are not likely in a perfunctory meeting once a year to raise the kind of question concerning investment policy that should be raised by a

192

board of trustees *representing beneficiaries* without waiting for an Advisory Council or the Congress to initiate change.

There appears to be a need, therefore, to encourage the board of trustees of social security funds to develop some degree of corporate life of its own. A first step would be to add two public members to the board from outside of the government. It should be the privilege of these or any other member of the board to submit annually separate statements to the Congress in regard to the financing of social security programs. Further, with the growing dimensions of social security operations and the need to give some substance to a trustee body representing a vast body of beneficiaries, it would not seem unreasonable to provide the board with a minimal staff. While not duplicating the work of the far larger administrative agencies, such a staff could assist the members of the board in their overall review of the financing of the social insurance program. No matter how responsible and dedicated administrative officers may be, it seems the counsel of wisdom to provide a mechanism for auditing their policies and operations when large funds are involved. This is particularly true when there can be some slight distinction between what is good for the general government and the general population and what is good for "the prospective beneficiaries of the program" and the millions already dependent upon it for their livelihood.

## CHAPTER XIV

# The Evolution and General Structure
# of Medicare

THE HISTORY OF THE DEVELOPMENT of health insurance in the United States is an example of the power of an obdurate and entrenched minority to hold back progress for the vast majority of a people. This entrenched minority has been not so much the thousands of individual physicians in this country who were too busy with their day-to-day practice of medicine to be concerned with the overall distribution of medical care, but, far more, the leaders they permitted to represent them at the various levels of "organized medicine," county, state, and national. The American Medical Association, instead of concentrating its efforts upon the advancement of the quality and availability of medical care for all, has spent vast energies and funds in fending off developments which would question their assumed prerogative to perpetuate a particular and profitable method of selling medical services. With little apparent interest over many years in increasing the supply of trained physicians to match increasing demand, the Association has helped to make the practice of medicine the most lucrative vocation in the country. Only recently has the Association broadened its concept of responsibility in respect to balancing the supply of physicians with the Nation's needs.

This may seem a harsh indictment of a professional association, but no analysis of the problem of the distribution of medical care in the United States could be honest unless it first indicated what has been the core of the problem. If one asks why legislation to protect our people against the hazards of dependent old age, premature death, and survivorship through national contributory social insurance has existed for a third of a century whereas, even yet, there is no parallel provision for the great majority of our people against the ever-present risks of ill-health, one cannot give any more accurate and significant reason than the persistent and effective opposition of organized medicine. Of course, there have been problems of administration and financing, but these could have been solved long ago if the medical profession, through its leaders, had accepted its proper obligation to cooperate in their solution.

Political activity in support of compulsory health insurance began as long ago as 1912 when the Progressive Party, with Theodore Roosevelt as its presidential candidate, supported it in its platform. During the ensuing few years, several state legislatures debated the issue of compulsory health insurance, and Congress held hearings on a federal plan. At that time, the American Medical Association looked favorably on the development as a means of improving medical care for wage earners. This statesmanlike posture was shortlived, however, and, by 1920, the tide had turned, and the A.M.A. had swung to a position of vigorous opposition to any system of compulsory health insurance, state or national. Its propaganda for years proclaimed the evils of "socialized medicine" with apparent disregard of the *social* obligation of a great profession to help solve a mounting *social* problem.*

* For an excellent and more detailed account of a half-century of political activity concerning national health insurance see

The Committee on Economic Security which recommended the establishment of national contributory old age insurance had a staff section assigned to develop measures for the improved means of providing for medical care. In the adverse climate of strong opposition by organized medicine, the staff of the section gave up in discouragement. While the opening sentence in the summary of staff reports reads, "No national program of economic security can be regarded in any sense as complete or effective without adequate provision for meeting the risks to security which arise out of ill health," there follows but a brief discussion of public health services.*

President Truman, members of Congress, the Social Security Board, and many groups fought valiantly during the late 1930's and throughout the 1940's to gain for the American people the same degree of protection against the risks of ill health that they had gained against the risks of dependent old age and survivorship, or unemployment. The American Medical Association, along with parallel professional associations, insurance carriers, and the Chamber of Commerce of the United States, was able, with large funds and persistent propaganda, to out-influence a cross-section of labor and consumer groups. President Truman made a last effort in 1950. President Eisenhower saw no need for compulsory health insurance.

During the 1950's, the campaign for health protection through compulsory social insurance took a new turn.

---

Herman M. and Anne R. Somers, *Medicare and the Hospitals, Issues and Prospects*, Washington, D.C.: 1967.

* *Social Security in America*, published for the Committee on Economic Security by the Social Security Board (Washington, D.C.: 1937), p. 35.

The mounting support for "social security" under OASDI provided a new vehicle, in political terms, of convincing Congress that social insurance was wanted by the people and that it was no terrible step toward a "socialized" world. The mounting costs of ill health were bearing down on old people with drastic results. A growing accumulation of studies, hearings, and conferences made this clear. By the early sixties, the argument for "insurance within insurance" for the protection of old age beneficiaries against the uncertain risks of the costs of ill health, magnified by age itself, became increasingly hard to refute.

With the election of President Kennedy in 1960, the pressure from the White House for health care for the aged mounted. President Johnson carried on. The crucial turning point came in President Johnson's landslide re-election in 1964. Health protection for the aged was a key issue in the campaign. Even the American Medical Association belatedly sensed the mounting demand of the voters for action on the issue. With the self-delusion which comes with years of clever delaying strategies, the Association tried the gambit of advancing a shoddy substitute for effective social insurance protection. They overplayed their hand.

Under the leadership of Wilbur Mills, the able and influential Chairman of the Ways and Means Committee of the House, in reaction to the vociferous complaints of the American Medical Association that *hospital* insurance was not enough, the Committee went beyond the recommendations of the Advisory Council on Social Security of January, 1965, for hospital insurance and added what became Part B of the Medicare program. This provided for the financing of doctors' services in addition to hospital care under Part A. A concession was made to the obsession of the Association against compulsory intervention by government by making coverage under Part B voluntary. The fact that 95 percent of the eligible aged soon chose to come under Part B demonstrated that the device of voluntary coverage was more a concession to the A.M.A. than a reflection of the will of the American people.

As enacted in 1965, the Medicare program provided for *hospital* insurance for the aged on a truly social insurance basis. The program was to be financed by funds derived from payroll taxes paid through working life. No premiums were required. Eligibility for benefits was integrated with that for cash benefits under old age insurance. The various types of benefits, the deductible amount, and the coinsurance features have been summarized in Chapter II. The provision for financing medical services, as contrasted to hospital services, was, however, not through a conventional social insurance mechanism, but rather by a governmentally operated form of assessment insurance lifted out of age-old and long-questioned mutual benefit experience. The costs of benefits were to be met year by year by premiums or assessments shared equally by the covered participants and the government. A saving feature was that the government contribution made voluntary coverage sufficiently attractive to reduce adverse selection. At the same time, it lessened to some degree the burden of the premiums upon the aged. It is of interest to note that this was the first time that Congress provided funds out of general revenues for direct medical care without a means test.

The foregoing brief summary of the fifty years of discussion and conflict which preceded the enactment of Medicare in 1965 will explain why the program is still an unfinished and internally fragmented mechanism. Unlike compulsory contributory old age insurance and the early addition of survivors insurance. Medicare is the creature of a half-century of infighting between those who saw a great national need and a small but powerful minority who wanted to preserve from any governmental intervention whatsoever an outmoded but lucrative method of doing their professional business. In contrast, in the development of old age insurance, there was no interest group of sufficient power to delay progress. The private insurance carriers were still a relatively small factor in providing old age security compared to the needs of millions of citizens. Their futile effort to contract out company coverage was more clever than wise, even in their own interest. State governments could offer little help to the aged without heavy federal subsidization. Meanwhile, a severe depression had stimulated a tremendous political drive for basic old age protection.

Neither the long history of delays and frustrations in the development of Medicare nor its shortcomings as an integrated and comprehensive system should lead one to discount its tremendous effect in affording a sense of security to the old people of the United States against the financial risks of illness. Almost all of the 20,500,000 people aged 65 and over in this country are now protected by hospital insurance under Part A of Medicare. About 19,500,000, or 95 percent of the aged, have medical insurance under Part B of Medicare. Over all, Medicare payments for hospital and physicians' care are estimated to account for 62 percent of the expenditures for hospital and physicians' services provided to the aged. Yet when *all* the health costs of old people, such as for drugs and other out-of-hospital needs, are included, the proportion of total health costs met by Medicare may be closer to 43 percent. The heavy costs of major illnesses are of deepest concern to the aged, however, and Medicare has gone far to lessen this concern.

In financial and administrative terms, Medicare has become a vast operation. Hospital insurance benefits in 1970 exceeded $4.5 billion, covering more than 7 million claims. These included payments for hospital services, extended care services, and home health care. Reimbursements for hospital services averaged $721. In 1970, bills for physicians' and related medical services reimbursed totaled $1.75 billion against charges of $2.4 billion, or a percentage reimbursement of 72.6. The number of doctors' bills processed approximated 40 million and averaged $61.

Before discussing the many issues involved in the improvement of the Medicare program, the key issue of its fragmented structure requires attention. There is no reasonable justification for separate insurance mechanisms for the financing of hospital services and the financing of medical services. Both involve professional and support personnel, as well as structures, equipment, and supplies. Effective and economical care today requires close coordination of a wide range of specialized activities which spread and overlap across the old boundaries of office, hospital, extended care, and out-patient and home treatment. The place, method, and means of treatment should be medically determined without the complication of diverse considerations of cost and compensation between programs. It is difficult enough to attain balance and coordination in a complex team operation without the arbitrary separation of one category of professional services from another.

The future development of effective distribution of health care will require a merging and averaging of costs over against the present "piece-rate," individualized pricing system which is a carryover of the days of the family doctor and his black bag. A medical event today can range from a single office call to a simple operation involving a dozen people to a serious and complex ailment requiring many specialists, intensive care, and expensive facilities. If social insurance is to provide the financing of medical care on an averaging actuarial basis, then the method of providing medical services must be developed on the basis of closely coordinated, interlocking, and balanced combinations of personnel and facilities which can be perfected to gain true quality and which can be financed without excessive cost. Only by such coordination can health insurance become more than a device for pouring more and more money into supporting an antiquated and wasteful system of delivery of health services.

When practically every other complex process of production or service in the country has been forced by the demand for *both* quality and economy to integrate operations within a carefully balanced and coordinated system in the use of costly manpower, facilities, and management, health services in the United States remain an amorphous collection of fragmented activities. Professional manpower is wasted by inefficient distribution and disorganized conditions as to best use, cooperation, and

201

compensation. Facilities and equipment are wasted, despite mounting costs, by maldistribution and antiquated methods of planning and administration. Effective and comprehensive delivery of health services is severely handicapped by built-in tensions increased by the unwillingness of professional personnel to recognize the requirements of integrated organization.

To make clear the present lack of integration in the organization of health services in this country one can compare the circumstances faced by a middle-income buyer in his purchase of a family automobile and of family health services for a period of time. In the former case, the buyer can visit several automobile agencies, receive full specifications concerning each car, try out alternative models, negotiate price and financing terms, and obtain appropriate guarantees and assurances of service. In the case of family health services, in contrast, he must put himself into the hands of one or more physicians who, on the onset of the illness of any member of the family, will determine *ex parte*, the amount of service required, the charges for the service, and the need for other specialists with their open-end charges. The charges made for professional services are not subject to normal market conditions in which a defined product or service is the object of competitive price negotiation; on the contrary, pricing, so far as the patient is concerned, is a onesided determination based on the doctor's personal estimate of the value of his services in the individual case or in general, influenced by a degree of local monopoly among the physicians available in a community or in a specialty.

The circumstances should a member of the buyer's

family enter a hospital become all the more complex and uncertain. The hospital, as a workshop for physicians, is strongly influenced in policy and operations by physicians who, however, usually take little if any responsibility for its costs or charges. Again the buyer becomes liable without any real determination on his part for a complex of tests, services, and supplies ordered by the doctor, but priced *ex parte* by the hospital or other physicians. The duration of a stay in the hospital is not for the purchaser to decide. He may be free to request a semi-private room or to order a television set or a telephone. While the hospital may control its "hotel service" costs, it, too, has no direct means of controlling the medical, laboratory, surgical, or other costs which the physician may incur on behalf of the patient.

In sum, once the purchaser of medical services embarks on the procedure he puts himself into the hands of second, third, or many other persons, without mutual responsibility on their part for total costs. It is as if the buyer of a car, after he drives it home, received a succession of bills from the makers of the engine, the body, the wheels, and other parts at prices they saw fit to charge regardless of the total combined cost to the purchaser, his ability to pay, or any competitive norm. The effect of such a lack of integration in the economy of the automobile industry is easy to imagine. Yet in his need for family health services, the American consumer has continued to be subject to the resistance of the medical profession to any general rationalization and integration in the health industry of the country. The great expansion of private and public health insurance has, as yet, served largely to divert more billions into an obsolete and dis-

203

organized system of distribution of medical and health care.

The effective integration of health services would no more undermine the *professional* responsibility or freedom of the medical profession than the age-old organization of universities has undermined the responsibility or freedom of faculty members. The scientific basis of the practice of medicine has been vastly enlarged by scientists organized and supported as members of coordinated faculties. Lawyers, engineers, and architects have increasingly found that modern professional practice involves the effective organization and integration of specialized personnel and support services. The medical profession has far too long sublimated a particular outmoded device of individual compensation into a vague theology which distorts clear thinking and prevents understanding cooperation in the advancement of the very goals to which their profession should be dedicated—the health of all their fellow men.

The basic reason for merging Parts A and B of Medicare is, therefore, the need to encourage, by every means possible, the integration of health services. The artificial device of separate financing of hospital and medical care under Medicare is an unfortunate historical accident which is one more obstacle to such integration. There are, however, other strong reasons for merging Parts A and B. The present method of financing Part B is itself antiquated. Voluntary assessment insurance schemes, over the long past, have a record of disaster. If experience is bad, premiums must be raised, good risks drop out, adverse risks stay in, premiums must then be increased even further, and the cycle repeats itself until the plan collapses. No assessment insurance program would seem to be more susceptible to the dangers of such adverse selection than one covering old people, with but limited funds for premiums, whose medical costs are sharply differentiated by relative age from 65 to 75 to 85. The present governmental contribution to Part B Medicare only attentuates the fundamental shortcomings of the voluntary assessment device it incorporates. Even with the government contribution, steadily rising premiums may lead to adverse selection through the hesitancy of younger and healthier retired persons to join the program.

The charging of a premium for necessary health protection as a deduction from a none-too-adequate old age benefit reflects more the hectic legislative history of Medicare than any *a priori* logic. To provide an old age benefit based on a lifetime of contribution and then take from it a variable current payment for universally needed health protection, when the aged beneficiary can least afford the charge, is a confused mixture of true social insurance and an assessment arrangement more appropriate to country clubs and real estate developments. The argument that a current voluntary premium is necessary in Part B of Medicare to assure individual responsibility appears to question the concept of *group* responsibility which underlies a compulsory contributory social insurance system. Control of use of physicians' services through specific deductibles and coinsurance requirements related to *individual* use, while burdensome on the poorer patient, is more effective and flexible than any common charge on all. In contrast, a current premium payment, especially when voluntary, encourages the notion that one should receive a return in service from time to time to get one's money's worth.

It is to be devoutly hoped that the historical accident of a bifurcated Medicare program will be repaired in the near future. A merger of Parts A and B into a single program with integrated financing will bring Medicare into the stream of logical evolution in a coordinated social insurance system. Health insurance, whether limited to the aged or not, involves concepts distinct from old age insurance. Even when the aberration of introducing assessments into the total system is corrected, the special features of health insurance as compared to those of cash benefit programs under OASDI will require years of experimentation before Medicare reaches the stage of maturity already attained by OASDI.

A basic feature of Medicare is that it uses the mechanism of compulsory contributory social insurance to provide not cash but a complex system of services. Under OASDI, when a cash benefit is paid, the program has completed its function, and it is the beneficiary's problem to make the money match his needs. Under Medicare, the system must go further and bear not only the risk of the contingency occurring but the risk of a wide range of costs in providing the services required. Limitations on meeting particular elements of cost such as through deductibles, coinsurance, or excluded services does not alter the main thrust that the program seeks primarily to deliver services and not cash.

The basic intent of the Medicare system to provide a *service* benefit rather than to indemnify the beneficiary for the cost of the service he has purchased has been most nearly fulfilled in respect to hospital services under Part A. In this case, the system has become a gigantic buyer of hospital services on behalf of its beneficiaries in an industry over which neither it nor any other integrated organization has any direct and positive control. Apart from the degree of utilization of hospital services which the individual physician determines in the individual case, the variation in hospital costs throughout the country and their pronounced upward trend has and will continue to require tremendous efforts on the part of the Social Security Administration and its intermediary agencies to rationalize. While in the early planning of Medicare emphasis was placed on deductibles and coinsurance as a means of controlling reimbursable hospital costs, experience has shown that the most fruitful means of savings is, rather, the close and constant overseeing of the managerial effectiveness of widely diverse institutions and the instructive process of auditing costs on a comparative basis. Compared to the total cost today of a stay in a hospital, the deductible has become a minor deterrent to unnecessary admissions. The far greater problem has become these total costs of justified admissions.

It is a serious handicap in the activities of the Social Security Administration and its intermediaries in rationalizing American hospital administration that they must limit their direct concern to services to the aged alone. It is a case of raising the level of a bed by lifting one of its legs. However, the person in the bed—the hospital management—has begun to realize that something is going on.

The intent of Medicare to provide a service benefit rather than indemnity insurance has, however, been frustrated to a marked degree by the unwillingness of American physicians to accept payment of Part B charges as determined under Medicare guidelines. The physicians of the country have insisted upon their longstanding prerogative of *ex parte* setting of charges when it is advantageous to them. In terms of control of the casual use of physicians' services and, therefore, the costs to the system, the deductible in respect to covered charges has probably had considerable effect. The rate of physicians' charges and their accumulation in cases of serious illness is a different matter. Here the Social Security Administration, its intermediaries, and, in turn, the patient, in respect to charges which Medicare refuses to meet, are faced with the obdurate resistance of the medical profession to any change from the business methods of a one-man enterprise in the nineteenth century.

Again, the charges claimed directly by the individual practitioner or by the beneficiary for indemnification have become the focus of an elaborate system of audit and analysis. The first effort has been to curtail abuse and excessive charges. The second is to develop the best prevailing norms in terms of appropriate charges for appropriate medical services in a wide variety of circumstances. It is fortunate that modern methods of computer record-keeping and analysis are now available to the insurance intermediaries which are the agents of the Social Security Administration in administering Medicare claims. As private carriers with long experience in claims procedures, their increasing efficiency in rationalizing such procedures and in controlling excessive charges cannot be censured as the operations of a monolithic government bureaucracy.

Despite its early resistance to Medicare, the medical profession has learned the simple lesson that, in business, an increased demand with a limited supply raises price. Medicare, by financing greatly needed medical services for the aged, has increased demand. By insisting on the free play of price among a limited number of individual competitors and refusal to cooperate in improved organization of services, the doctors have done extremely well. The most lucrative profession is becoming more and more lucrative, and the old people of the country are paying higher and higher premiums deducted from their barely sufficient benefits.

The lack of effective organization of health services in the United States affects far more than the costs of physicians' services. The hospital is essentially an extension of the doctor's office, a workshop provided by the community to assist him in curing the sick. It is the doctor who controls admissions, who directs treatment, and who arranges discharges. Therefore, the control of the availability, quality, and duration of hospital service is largely in his hands. If the physician looks upon Medicare merely as a bill-paying agency rather than as an essential part of an integrated health-delivery system, progress will be slow in assuring effective care for all at costs which the people can afford. In the following chapter, we will outline the steps which will be required to overcome the more immediate shortcomings of Medicare and to prepare the way for a more comprehensive program of health insurance in the United States.

## CHAPTER XV

# Health Care: The Expanding Frontier of
# Social Security

As ONE REVIEWS the history of social security in the
United States, it becomes obvious that in one of the
most important areas of human need, that for adequate
health services, we have introduced social insurance by
the back door. Instead of attacking the need for the insured sharing of risks of health costs for all of our citizens, we have, after a prodigious effort, succeeded in
securing partial protection for our old people against
these risks by a bifurcated, clumsily financed system of
Medicare. The needs of the old for health protection had
become all too obvious. Cash benefits under OASDI were
far too low to absorb the shock of large and sudden medical costs. We needed to provide "insurance within insurance" to make old age protection sufficient to give a real
sense of security to our people. In developing Medicare,
however, we have found ourselves facing a whole range
of problems which are equally relevant to general health
insurance for the total population. On an even wider
scale, we have come to a clear recognition of the limits
of the mechanism of contributory social insurance, standing alone, in meeting the full range of costs arising from
the susceptibility of the human organism to disease, injury, and deterioration.

It seems best at this point in our discussion to consider
the next steps in the improvement of what we have, Medicare, and to define its limits in providing for the care of

the aged. Some of the limiting conditions will relate to the fact that it is social insurance, covering only insurable risks, and financed on an inadequate basis. Other limiting conditions will relate to proper areas of coverage within a system still related to long-continued loss of earnings. An even more serious problem will be the mounting costs of the system in the face of a poorly organized, unintegrated system of distribution of medical care. By clarifying the issues and problems in the extension and improvement of what we have, we can more effectively address ourselves to the larger problem of providing health care to our total population through contributory health insurance or through other means.

In this step-by-step plan of attack, an immediate and practical question is: Is the protection now provided to aged beneficiaries by Medicare adequate? Relative adequacy involves questions of limitations on services compensated, such as deductibles and coinsurance; duration limits; and eligibility for particular services. It also concerns the degree of coverage of total health needs such as out-of-hospital drugs, dental services, and optical services and supplies.

The deductible for hospital services under Part A Medicare was introduced for two reasons: to discourage casual and unnecessary admissions and to save money for the system. It was set at approximately one day's charge for hospital service. Starting at $40 in 1965, it has risen in 1971 to $60. While it is difficult to assess the effect of this deductible in controlling admissions, there is reason to believe that the far greater unmet costs attending the usual stay in a hospital have been far more important than the deductible in discouraging unnecessary admissions.

211

The deductible has become, in fact, primarily a cost-saving device for the system. The issue becomes, therefore, whether costs of hospital care for the aged should be borne by them from concurrent cash old age insurance benefits or other limited resources, or whether it should be financed from contributions of the beneficiary during his working life, by his employers, or by the government.

It can be argued that the concurrent payment of a part of the cost of hospitalization may encourage a wholesome sense of participation in costs on the part of the patient. But this argument must be assessed in terms of the *total* costs incurred by him in the period of illness, including coinsurance and possible unmet hospital costs, deductibles and coinsurance for physicians' services, out-of-hospital expenses during recovery, and loss of potential earnings. In sum, the justification for a deductible under hospital insurance must be weighed in terms of the total costs of an illness to a patient of limited means, and what he can afford to pay.

As the deductible for hospital charges under Part A of Medicare has risen from $40 to $60 and threatens to increase steadily under the present formula, there is strong reason to reopen the whole question of the justification of both the principle and the specific determination of deductibles, particularly in the case of the total complex of hospital charges. A social insurance mechanism should implement the basic function of spreading risks in the way that they can be best borne within reasonable limits of cost to the contributors or to the government. It should not be diverted by the desire for bookkeeping neatness of a formula based on secondary considerations. The test of adequacy in social insurance benefits is the imputed need of the beneficiary in the light of predetermined conditions, not administrative or financial convenience. There is good reason to suggest that the deductible under hospital insurance (Part A of Medicare) remain fixed at the present level of $60 in the years to come, regardless of mounting hospital costs. At most, upward charges should be limited to the same proportion by which cash OASDI benefits increase, since in many cases this will be the main source of funds used to meet the deductible.

The coinsurance requirements under hospital insurance under Medicare are now a direct proportion of the deductible amount. From the 61st through the 90th day in a spell of illness, one-fourth of the deductible amount ($15 in 1971) is charged to the patient per day. The same considerations of social insurance policy are relevant in setting this coinsurance amount as in the case of the deductible. It has been argued in this case, however, that the coinsurance charge helps in controlling the length of stay in the hospital. In the face of mounting hospital costs, the temptation has become strong to control the costs to the insurance system by shifting costs to the patient. If it is true that patients are staying too long in hospitals, which has not been proved, the proper approach is through the improvement of the effectiveness of utilization review committees of physicians who can determine the medical needs of the *individual* patient, or by increasing the availability of adequate nursing homes, rather than through adding to the already heavy costs of the patient who needs protracted hospital care. Again, it is not sound social insurance policy to fail to meet imputed needs by resort to mechanistic, cost-saving devices.

213

The limit of 90 days of hospital service under Part A Medicare in a single spell of illness has been tempered by the establishment of a life-reserve eligibility of 60 additional days. The advantage of the life reserve has been reduced, however, by the requirement of a heavy coinsurance charge of $30 a day. The Advisory Council of 1969-71 recommended that the life reserve be doubled to 120 days and that the coinsurance be reduced to $15 a day. In the face of the heavy medical costs incurred by an old person in a final or other very serious illness, the Council's recommendation appears fully justified. The fear of a long and costly final illness haunts many old people. To end one's life as a ward of the state, or to drain the resources of one's children, is an all-too-frequent prospect for old persons in America. Only an adequate social insurance program can alleviate this fear.

It remains true, however, that a contributory social insurance program must operate on the basis of defined and measurable contingencies as well as within reasonable limits of cost relative to those of other socially needed services. The limits of 90 days on normal hospital stays and 120 days as a life reserve seem reasonable outside limits upon insurable risk. Even though reached in rare instances, these limits afford a valuable sense of security. They may have some salutary effect in encouraging economy in hospital use if the medical profession fails to exercise fully its proper responsibility in conserving hospital services for those who need them. The major issue appears to be, therefore, the extent to which coinsurance has been used as a cost-saving device to the impairment of adequate protection of the patient under effective social insurance.

214

The provisions for service in extended care facilities under hospital insurance (Part A of Medicare) involve many of the same considerations as those which have been discussed in respect to service in the general hospital. Under present legislation, the patient who has spent at least 3 days in a hospital may be covered for 100 days in an extended care facility (essentially a skilled nursing home), or in a special area of the hospital designated as an extended care facility, in any benefit period. A coinsurance charge of $7.50 a day is made after the first 20 days. From the point of view of adequacy of protection under social insurance, the major question is whether a life reserve should not be added to the 100 days of regular coverage. An even more important problem, however, is the increase in the availability of adequate facilities. Whether the restriction that three days must be spent in a hospital before a patient is eligible for compensated extended care services is necessary should be studied in the light of experience. It is, again, a device developed in the early planning of a new program and subject to the overall standards of adequate protection.

The deductible under *medical* insurance (Part B of Medicare) involves considerations which are different, at least in degree, from those involved in hospital insurance. The admission to a hospital is a major event in the life of an old person and involves a complex of costs of uncertain proportions. The degree of illness is likely to be obvious to all concerned. A visit to a doctor's office, however, can be more casual, discretionary, and psychologically satisfying. Also, the number of patients a doctor can see in his office varies widely, with a concomitant variation in possible income. With the incidence of an office call and its repetition so much a reflection of individual predispositions, both of patients and of doctors, departures from a medically justifiable norm of frequency in office calls are more likely than excesses in hospital admissions. While some old people may go to the doctor too often, others may delay going too long. On the part of the doctor, however, the long-established piece-rate method of charging for service in his office (or on hospital rounds) lends itself to a rapid accumulation of income under modern conditions of secretaries, insurance benefits, and concern for health which the small-town doctor of past years, visiting patients in widely separated homes, would have considered fabulous.

In the light of these factors in medical practice today, it does not seem unreasonable to place some restraint on the free use of *medical* services, especially outside of the hospital. The simplest restraint is a monetary charge. It tends to limit the patient, and through him the doctor, to the number of contacts which may be more reasonably justified in medical terms. It is, however, but a partial and somewhat inefficient restraint. It may discourage early diagnosis and preventive counseling. A far more effective restraint will always be the professional responsibility of the doctor in using his time and skills to the best advantage of all those who truly need his help in the prevention and cure of disabling illness.

The deductible for medical services under health insurance (Part B of Medicare) is the first $50 in any year. The coinsurance requirement is 20 percent. Both are related, however, to the "reasonable charges" determined by the Medicare administration. If a doctor is unwilling to accept as fee the "reasonable charge" as determined under Medicare guidelines, the patient may pay far more than 80 percent of charges after the first $50 in a year. If it were not for this fact, it would be difficult to argue against the present deductible and coinsurance requirements. But this does not mean that the Medicare program is adequately relieving the old of the burden of professional medical costs so long as actual charges for medical services may be far larger.

The answer to the problem of unmet doctors' bills beyond the requirements of the deductible and coinsurance cannot be provided by altering these requirements. It is involved, rather, in the far greater problem of developing an effective distribution of health care. This will be discussed later. However, from the point of view of the Medicare administration, charges to patients *within* the reimbursable limits may become excessive through too frequent calls or other unnecessary services. The control of these aberrations from norm requires the constant improvement of administrative oversight by the Social Security Administration and its intermediaries. But even the best of administration cannot overcome the built-in inefficiency of an obsolete system of distribution of medical care. This will require fundamental change before any system of social insurance can be fully effective in precisely matching its benefits to the proper needs of its beneficiaries.

An important gap in Medicare's coverage of the health costs of the aged is the lack of reimbursement of expenditures for prescription drugs purchased outside of the hospital and not a part of a doctor's in-office treatment. Based on the special needs of many old people for continuing medication for ailments accentuated by age, it is estimated that 20 percent of their health expenditures are for prescription drugs or other medically required supplies. The annual cost for such drugs for persons over 65 is more than three times those for younger persons. The annual expenditures for drugs for the severely disabled of all ages are six times those for the population as a whole.

The administrative problems and financial costs of covering out-of-hospital prescription drugs have received intensive study over several years. The Advisory Council of 1969-71 recommended such coverage, but assumed that some time would be required to develop the administrative procedures necessary. It preferred a comprehensive inclusion of the many kinds of prescription drugs needed, rather than any limited list. To control excessive use and costs, it recommended a system of co-payment, that is a payment by the beneficiary of $2 for each new prescription and $1 for each refilling of the same prescription, rather than an annual deductible amount or a percentage coinsurance. The Council believed that this method of co-payment would relieve the beneficiary of burdensome record-keeping and would simplify administration generally. An added advantage is that the cost to the beneficiary is kept within reasonable limits even though costly drugs are involved. Under the Council's plan, the major administrative task would center in the vendor, who would claim from the Medicare administration reimbursement for the reasonable net cost of drugs furnished and for the service rendered. With vast numbers of purchases involved, the large number of vendors, and the problems of pricing, proper distribution, and quality, the administrative burden on the Social Security Administration would still be heavy.

On balance, the needs of the old people of the country warrant an early extension of Medicare to cover out-of-hospital prescription drugs. The cost of such coverage was estimated by the Advisory Council to approximate an addition of 0.47 percent in a combined employer-employee payroll tax. This included coverage of younger disabled beneficiaries whose drug costs far exceed those of the aged. More important than costs in the timing of the introduction of out-of-hospital drug coverage is, however, the need to work out effective administrative machinery. This major cost is already being met by many older citizens at a time in life when they are least able to afford it.

The questions of cost and administration in the coverage of additional benefits, such as dental services, for the aged under Medicare run parallel to those already outlined. In the balancing of the protective coverage of a total social insurance program, there are reasonable limits in the extension of one means of help over against all others. So long as millions of young people have no social insurance protection against major health costs, it seems out of proportion to add features of less pressing importance in the care of the aged.

Just as cash benefits under the Social Security Act were, after a long delay, broadened to cover persons with long-continuing disabilities, it is assumed that Medicare benefits should be similarly broadened, ideally with far less delay. The parallel extensions of coverage follow a common logic that contributory social insurance is the most effective way to protect normally employed persons, and their dependents, against the financial risks involved in permanent or long-continued loss of earnings because

219

of personal incapacity for normal employment. The disabled need not only cash benefits but, even more than the aged, some means of meeting their extraordinary medical expenses. The Advisory Council of 1969-71 found that, in 1965, 29 percent of the disabled were hospitalized compared to 14 percent of the aged; that the disabled stay in the hospital twice as long; and that a higher proportion have out-of-hospital visits to their physicians. Further, disabled persons have severely limited incomes since they can do little, if any work, and may have used up their savings. Most are unable to afford adequate private health insurance protection. The Council recommended Medicare coverage for disabled workers, disabled widows and disabled dependent widowers, disabled wives and disabled dependent husbands of social security beneficiaries, and people aged 18 or over who receive social security benefits because they became disabled before reaching age 22.*

Emphasizing the costs involved, the Council did not recommend Medicare benefits for the dependents of disabled beneficiaries where the dependent person was not disabled. While it might be assumed that such dependents could obtain protection through private or, eventually, general public health insurance, the exclusion of these dependents from Medicare protection is debatable in terms of the present adequacy of the system. If Medicare coverage is a logical adjunct to OASDI coverage when earnings stop because of physical impairment in old age *and* an aged wife is then covered, should not the young

*Reports of the 1971 Advisory Council on Social Security, p. 50. House Document 92-80, 92nd Congress, 1st Session. Washington: U.S. Printing Office.

wife and children of a physically impaired beneficiary be protected? The nub of the distinction is not the logic of adequacy, however, but a hesitancy to enter still further into the area of *general* health insurance in covering under Medicare anyone who is neither old nor permanently disabled. If the wives and children of *disabled* beneficiaries were protected under Medicare, why not cover widows and children receiving *survivors* benefits? The issue makes clear the fact that health insurance in the United States is in in a transitional stage. We are only now recognizing the costs involved in a comprehensive system of health protection under social insurance. We have entered the American home through the back door to protect the old people in the kitchen, but hesitate to move on into the living room to protect the rest of the family.

But even with the old people, Medicare stops short of protecting them in a most vulnerable stage of life, the period of declining capacity, physical or mental, when the old person cannot take care of himself and yet is not undergoing medical treatment. This is the problem of *custodial* care. With increasing longevity and the physical, economic, and domestic arrangements of modern urban and suburban living, the problem of care for the physically or mentally impaired old person has become critical for the aged person himself and for his family, if any survives. Medicare, as the name implies, is intended to provide medical service, not custodial care. It cannot spread over into custodial care without becoming involved in serious problems of finance, facilities, eligibility, and administration. Even more fundamental, it would be moving outside the bounds of effective use of the instrument of contributory social insurance.

221

To be insurable, a contingency must be beyond the control of the insured or of those responsible for him. Apart from the need for sustained medical treatment, the reasons for providing institutional custodial care for one old person rather than another would be difficult to justify since the attitudes, interests, resources, and sense of responsibility of the persons involved and their families would be controlling factors. The highly discretionary decision to finance custodial care for an impaired and needy old person falls properly in the area of public assistance and not in that of a contributory social insurance system which must be limited to clearly defined, insurable risks.

The remedy for the serious lack of adequate custodial care for the impaired aged in this country, whether in institutions or in the home, is a greatly improved system of facilities and services subsidized, where necessary, by public funds. Subject to minimal standards, such facilities and services should range in level of service and cost in relation to individual needs and means, including, but not limited to, old age insurance benefits. The choice whether to enter a residential institution, to depend upon homemaker services, or to rely upon one's family for care would be far easier if, by public concern and investment, our whole system of care for persons chronically impaired by age were lifted out of its present deplorable state. The costs of institutional care for the middle-income aged has become a critical burden on many families. For the poor, the character of institutional care is often disgraceful, in the richest country in the world.

The problems of financing an adequate system of Medicare are so much involved in the parallel problems of financing the OASDI system that they have been covered in earlier chapters. It should be emphasized again, however, that in terms of both sound social insurance philosophy and practical necessity a three-way sharing of costs by the employer, employee, and the government will be essential to the effective development of social insurance in this country. This is already clearly evident in the case of Medicare with its steadily mounting outlays. The reasons for this conclusion need not be repeated here. The original planners of the old age insurance system saw clearly in 1934-35 the need for a broad base of financial support. The Advisory Council of 1969-71, thirty-five years later, renewed the recommendation for such support in the case of Medicare. An enlargement of our social insurance system to cover general health care without a three-way sharing of costs—employer, employee, and government—would be unwise, even if it were possible.

Even more than a clarification of financial policy, an enlargement of our social insurance system to cover general health care will require a radical reorganization of our national system of distributing health services. The shortcomings of the present system have been discussed. To attain the radical reorganization necessary to avoid pouring more and more billions of dollars into an obsolete system will require a change in the economic structure of the whole health service complex, in the means by which medical and supporting manpower are developed and compensated, and in the control, financing, and administration of hospitals and other health facilities and services. The degree of change required may seem heroic, but only because change, like a dammed-up river, has been held back far too long. While other systems of production and service in America have evolved steadily, the health industry, in its system of distribution, has treasured the attributes of a Victorian tailor shop.

To outline in any detail an effective economic and administrative structure for the health industry of the United States is beyond the function of a book on social insurance philosophy. Further, it would be foolish to define arrangements which only experience will prove workable. It may be both fair and helpful, however, to suggest the basic principles of a system of health services with which Medicare or any more general system of social insurance could cooperate in relieving the American people of the risks of insecurity through ill health.

The basic requirement of such a model system of health services is the close coordination of all general services related to the prevention and cure of illness into a single continuum in which the doctor, the hospital, the extended care facility, and the homecare services are integrated parts of a single overall organization, community by community. The natural core of such an organization is the community medical center and, within it, the hospital and clinic as the workshop of the medical practitioner and the professional and paraprofessional personnel associated with him. The essential function of this integrated organization is to provide the highest quality of health service at the most reasonable *average* economic cost per member of the community.

Because of the wide variation in the cost of the treatment of diverse ailments, the averaging of costs over the group served should be done by the integrated health service organization, not by any health insurance program. The reason for this is fundamental to sound organization and sound economics. It is the health center which must plan for the proper balance of trained manpower at all levels throughout a wide range of specializations. It is also the health center which must plan the development of plant, facilities, and equipment to get the best cost-effectiveness balance in the curing of the sick. The provision of a service or the administration of function without a sense of economy leads to sloppiness and eventual deterioration in any profession, business, or art. The practice of medicine is no exception. By bringing together the demanding but necessary responsibility for economic as well as medical planning into the integrated health center, the complex strategy of raising the level of health of all of our people would be in the hands of those who can effectively determine and implement it.

The model plan outlined requires that the medical profession of this country fully assume two major responsibilities which they have long sought to avoid, in principle, even though they have assumed them to some degree, in fact. The first is the responsibility, in full partnership with lay members of boards and administrators, for the total economy of an integrated medical center, as well as of its total medical service. The second is the responsibility to determine their own compensation as a reasonable segment of the total income available to the medical center from all appropriate sources. This assumes that the income of the medical center is not made up of casual fees and charges, but rather of a combined flow of payments related, per capita, to the body of persons eligible for the health services provided. The major change in the compensation of the individual doctor is that differentials in compensation would be determined by appropriate quasi-judicial committees of his peers, within a total fund available, and not by his *ex parte* decision, as an individual entrepreneur.

Since the method of compensating doctors is of so much a concern to organized medicine in this country, a few additional comments seem appropriate in even a broad-brush outline. The administrative method of determining professional and executive compensation through the use of competent personnel committees, operating within budgetary limits, runs through the vast range of the more effective corporate organizations and institutions of the country. The precise device of payment is secondary to the judicious determination of the contribution of the individual. Differentials may be wide so long as the total of compensation for the category covered falls within reasonable proportion to that of all other manpower and to all other costs. An example which may be helpful is that in the compensation of a university faculty there are differentials ranging from that for a Nobel laureate in physics to that of an instructor in English or of a janitor. The key fact is that the differentials are determined by means of a thorough and judicious evaluation procedure, implemented by persons of high and relevant competency, operating within limits set by the total economy of the university.

The steps in the evolution of a system of integrated health centers, community by community in the United States, involve the highest order of intelligence, judgment, imagination, and dedication on the part of a wide range of community and national leaders. Most of all, they require a fundamentally revised conception on the part of the medical profession of the country of their role and obligation in attaining their proper goal, a high quality of health care for all our people. The complex administrative organization and the vast financial costs required for modern health services will inevitably force a change in the system of distribution of health care. If the medical profession insists upon holding back the change in order to preserve an obsolete and lucrative system of personal compensation, they will lose the great opportunity to help guide change constructively toward one of the finest health services in the world and will drift into the category of hired employees of a state-administered medical service. Such a narrow view of professional obligation, both individually and collectively, would be the relinquishment of a birthright of leadership for a mess of bureaucratic pottage.

The further development of Medicare involves many problems. The implementation of the lessons learned under Medicare in the development of *general* health insurance for all will involve many more. The greatest problem in both is an obsolete and disorganized national system of distribution of health care. The social insurance problems of *financing* the average per capita costs of adequate medical care for all could be readily mastered if the leaders of the medical profession of the country would cooperate in the reorganization of the health services to be financed. Without such reorganization, a critical area in the protection of our people through social insurance will remain beyond our reach.

# CHAPTER XVI

## The Essentials of an Effective Program for
## Social Security in the United States

SINCE THE GREAT DEPRESSION of the early 1930's, the United States has moved a long way in developing an effective national system of social security. It still has a long way to go. In the progress of organized societies, the past *is* prologue for the future. It is well to sharpen up the lessons learned in the past in order to apply them to the future. The most important lessons learned from the past are those which define a philosophy. A tested and consistent philosophy is the basis of sound and effective policy. In no area of national concern is this truth more evident than in building a system of social security for a nation of over two hundred million people.

We have learned that the American people want a system of protection against the major economic risks of life which will provide such protection as a matter of right and not of charity, no matter how carefully disguised. They are willing to contribute a considerable proportion of their current earnings to assure that protection. Further, they believe that the system should be as universal as possible and protect everyone, rich or poor, throughout the country, related to a certain segment of earned income. Seeing the system as a social mechanism operated by government, they recognize that lower-income persons need a larger benefit proportional to normal earnings under that system than higher-income people do. They thus accept a socially determined degree of redistribution

228

of income within the system in order to provide more effectively for *basic* human needs. At the same time, they believe that benefits should reflect, in reasonable degree, the differential contribution of the beneficiary to a society which depends upon the sustained incentive and attainment of its members.

Subject to this concept of graduated benefits, where these are in the form of cash, the American people support a progressive evolution of a contributory social insurance system toward the goal of *adequate* coverage of the major risks faced by the family unit. They recognize the need to provide against dependency in old age, on the part of survivors, or where serious disability at any age prevents self-sufficiency. When benefits are in the form of service, such as health care, they support the concept that all eligible beneficiaries should receive the same quality and amount of protection, regardless of past earnings. It is, further, a fair estimate of American opinion that it favors health service benefits under contributory insurance for all persons now receiving cash benefits under the social insurance system and, as soon as possible, for all persons participating as contributors to that system, and for their families as well.

If these are the aspirations of the American people, certain principles evolve in the appropriate response of government. First, to finance such a system of protection as a matter of right, the government must require a schedule of compulsory contributions, not only on the part of potential beneficiaries, but also on the part of their employers. It must sustain a system of redistribution of current flows of national income as between contributors and beneficiaries (or those who serve them) which

229

will be adequate to meet assumed obligations and, at the same time, not cause disruption of the normal fiscal operations of the government. It must avoid the accumulation of vast reserves which deflate the economy. It must, however, plan the income and disbursements of the social insurance system to assure a reasonable contingency fund to absorb unexpected fluctuations in either income or outgo.

Further, it is the obligation of government, in introducing a contributory social insurance system, to avoid thrusting upon it burdens in the amelioration or prevention of dependency for which the system is not properly financed or for which it is not designed. Since social insurance involves, through graduations in cash benefits and in a common level of health service benefits, a very considerable degree of social redistribution of income, it is a sound principle that the government should share in the total cost of the system. The general justification of such participation is the greater where, in the start of a system or of any of its components, a program financed by employer and employee contributions is called upon to absorb the cost of benefits for persons already old. Further, the government must avoid thrusting upon a contributory social insurance system the cost of supporting persons of insufficient earnings under the system to warrant eligibility for benefits. A distortion of purpose may also arise through unreasonably liberal eligibility requirements or arbitrarily high minimum benefits.

To prevent the impairment of the integrity and effectiveness of a national system of contributory social insurance by the inclusion of noninsurable risks, the government should undergird the social insurance system by a national system of public assistance. To perform its proper role both in the protection of our citizens and in the undergirding of the social insurance system, the national system of public assistance should be wholly integrated in structure, federally financed, and federally administered. It should be staffed by personnel of professional competency, operating under common national standards yet sensitive to local and individual needs. Only by the combination of the two complementary systems, national contributory social insurance and national public assistance, operating with efficiency, humane understanding, and appropriate adjustment to the American economy, can the social security of our people be assured.

The Old Age, Survivors and Disability Insurance program of the country reflects the maturing process of a generation of evolution. Further justified improvements have been discussed in detail in the preceding chapters. As a relatively new endeavor, however, the introduction of contributory social insurance into the area of health care has made evident several major issues in national social security philosophy and policy. If adequate health care is the right of every citizen, then our system of distribution of health care must be fundamentally restructured. Contributory social insurance should not be used to finance, wastefully and ineffectively, an obsolete system of health services. Further, a system of protection in the financing of health services, whether Medicare or a general health insurance program, should itself be an integrated system to coordinate with an integrated system of health distribution. The merger of Parts A and B of Medicare is immediately required.

231

The introduction of Medicare, in particular, has brought to the surface the general principle of government participation in the financing of contributory social insurance recognized by those who planned the system in 1934-35. With the large degree of social redistribution of income between the working population and those already old when Medicare began, and between higher-income contributors and lower-income contributors currently receiving the same protection, the justification of an immediate three-way equal sharing of the costs of the Medicare, as a whole, has become increasingly clear. The proper coverage of the disabled under Medicare would further justify the change. If still further reason is needed, the cost of improvements in the scope of Medicare protection in terms of services and supplies covered, in the duration of services, and in the avoidance of unreasonable coinsurance requirements should not be thrust upon a limited source of financing—payroll taxes.

Only by the thorough revaluation of our experience under Medicare and the courageous efforts of government in bringing about the restructuring of our system of distribution of health care will the ground be laid for an extension of contributory social insurance to protect all our citizens against the mounting cost of adequate health care. Such care has come to be too essential an element in the security of our people to be left to a disordered, uncertain, and costly combination of public relief, private insurance, and great individual risk. There are many indications that our people want adequate health care as a matter of right and are willing to pay their share of costs under a rationalized system of financing. The critical obstacle in the provision of adequate health care is not

232

problems in the development of effective financing under contributory social insurance, but the long-continued opposition of a privileged profession which seems more concerned in preserving obsolete methods of compensation than in cooperating with the rest of society in reorganizing a great and essential service.

With the cooperation of the medical profession, the problems of developing integrated health centers could be solved. The ingenuity of Americans in creating effective, integrated institutions in supplying other essential goods and services would be readily available if the medical profession would look to the future rather than the past. Without vision on the part of that profession, the mounting public demand for an adequate system of health care may shift its focus from contributory social insurance for financing alone to public medicine, financed through general taxation and administered by the state.

Little has been said here about the future of unemployment insurance in the United States. Many of the principles discussed throughout this book apply to this form of social insurance. It is my conviction now, as in 1934, that unemployment insurance should be an integrated element of a *national* system of social security. Only by such a radical change in structure can the essential principles of sound social insurance policy be implemented. I have little hope that the errors of the past will be corrected in my time. As for workmen's compensation insurance, I am convinced that its traditions are so far removed from those of sound social insurance that I leave it to the prayerful concern of others.

# Appendix

## Selected Readings on Social Security Philosophy and Policy in the United States

THE LITERATURE on social security has grown at a geometric rate of increase over the past forty years. Despite its selectivity, the last edition of *Basic Readings in Social Security* published by the Social Security Administration in 1970 runs to 181 pages. The specialist will find the bibliography invaluable; the general reader will be overwhelmed. To help the latter who seeks further background or differing points of view on American experience and philosophy, a short annotated reading list of books and official documents follows. The coverage emphasizes the development of the federally administered programs of Old Age, Survivors and Disability Insurance (OASDI) and Medicare. Further, to save the reader's time, the early, formative period and current issues in policy are emphasized, leaving to the *Basic Readings* bibliography the coverage of hundreds of official documents, specialized articles, and current studies published in the intervening years.

### I. HISTORICAL DEVELOPMENT

(a) *Early Background*

Armstrong, Barbara N. *Insuring the Essentials, Minimum Wage plus Social Insurance—A Living Wage Program.* New York: Macmillan, 1932.

Epstein, Abraham. *Insecurity, A Challenge to America: A Study of Social Insurance in the United States and Abroad.* Rev. Ed. New York: Agathon Press, Inc., 1968.

Rubinow, I. M. *The Quest for Security*. New York: Henry Holt, 1934.

These three books are by authors who were influential in the earliest formative stage in the development of American old age security. Mrs. Armstrong, as staff member of the Committee on Economic Security in 1934-35, took a leading part in planning the original program. Abraham Epstein was an indefatigable proponent of old age security in the 1920's and 1930's. It is said that it was Rubinow's book, published in 1934, which enhanced President Roosevelt's interest in social security.

(b) *The Crucial Period: 1934-39*

Altmeyer, Arthur J. *The Formative Years of Social Security*. Madison: University of Wisconsin Press, 1966.

Committee on Economic Security. *Social Security in America: The Factual Background of the Social Security Act as Summarized from Staff Reports to the Committee on Economic Security*. (Social Security Board Publication No. 20.) Washington: U.S. G. P. O., 1937.

Douglas, Paul H. *Social Security in the United States: An Analysis and Appraisal of the Federal Social Security Act*. 2nd ed. New York: McGraw-Hill Book Company, Inc., 1939.

Holtzman, Abraham, *The Townsend Movement: A Political Study*. New York: Bookman Associates, 1963.

Schlabach, Theron F. *Edwin E. Witte: Cautious Reformer*. Madison: Wisconsin State Historical Society of Wisconsin, 1969.

Witte, Edwin S. *The Development of the Social Security Act: A Memorandum on the History of the Committee on Economic Security and Drafting and Legislative History of the Social Security Act*. Madison: University of Wisconsin Press, 1962.

Arthur Altmeyer not only participated in the planning of the Social Security Act but, as chairman of the Social Security Board, was long the leader in the development of the social security program. Edwin Witte was director of the staff of the Committee on Economic Security in 1934-35 and a member of the first Advisory Council of 1937-38. His detailed account of the events of 1934-35 was published after his death. The reports of the staff of the Committee on Economic Security are of interest in indicating much of the factual background on which the original planning of the program was based. Paul Douglas' contemporary account of the early period is more valuable because of his participation in the first Advisory Council. Schlabach's narrative of Witte's participation in the development of old age insurance supplements the author's account in Chapter I. Holtzman's book on the Townsend Movement makes clear the political pressure under which Congress was operating in 1935.

(c) *Congressional Enactment and Court Approval*

U.S. Congress. House. Committee on Ways and Means. *Economic Security Act.* Hearings on H.R. 4120, a bill to alleviate the hazards of old age, unemployment, illness and dependency, to establish a social insurance board in the Department of Labor, to raise revenue, and for other purposes. (74th Cong., 1st sess.) Washington: U.S. G. P. O., 1935.

U.S. Congress. House. *The Social Security Bill.* A report to accompany H.R. 7260. (75th Cong., 1st sess., H. Rept. 615.) Washington: U.S. G. P. O., 1935.

U.S. Congress. Senate. Committee on Finance. *Economic Security Act.* Hearings on S. 1130, a bill to alleviate the hazards of old age, unemployment, illness, and dependency, to establish a social insurance board in the Department of Labor, to raise revenue, and for other purposes. (74th Cong., 1st sess.) Washington: U.S. G. P. O., 1935.

U.S. Congress. Senate. *The Social Security Bill.* A report to accompany H.R. 7260. (74th Cong., 1st sess., S. Rept. 628.) Washington: U.S. G. P. O., 1935.

U.S. Supreme Court. *Arguments in the Cases Arising Under the Social Security Act and the Alabama Unemployment Compensation Law, April 7-9, 1937.* (75th Cong., 1st sess., S. Doc. 53.) Washington: U.S. G. P. O., 1937.

U.S. Supreme Court. *The Constitutionality of the Social Security Act.* Opinions of the Supreme Court in the cases involving the constitutionality of the Social Security Act: Charles C. Steward Machine Company *v.* Harwell G. Davis, individually and as Collector of Internal Revenue for the District of Alabama, May 26, 1937. (75th Cong., 1st sess. S. Doc. 74.) Washington: U.S. G. P. O., 1937.

These official documents, while too extensive for more than cursory review, afford a rich source of evidence on the political and legal milieu in which the American social security program was first enacted and constitutionally justified. For the long series of Congressional Hearings and reports over the years, see *Basic Readings in Social Security*, cited above.

(d) *Reports of Advisory Councils on Social Security*

U. S. Advisory Council on Social Security. *Final Report.* U.S. G. P. O., 1939.

U.S. Advisory Council on Social Security. *Report on Old Age and Survivors Insurance.* (80th Cong., 2nd sess., S. Doc. 149.) Washington: U.S. G. P. O., 1948.

U.S. Advisory Council on Social Security. *Report on Permanent and Total Disability Insurance.* (80th Cong., 2nd. sess., S. Doc. 162.) Washington: U.S. G. P. O., 1948.

U.S. Advisory Council on Social Security Financing. *Financing Old-Age, Survivors and Disability Insurance: A Report.* Washington: U.S. G. P. O., 1960.

U.S. Advisory Council on Social Security. *The Status of the Social Security Program and Recommendations for its Improvement: A Report.* Washington: U.S. G. P. O., 1965.

U.S. Advisory Council on Social Security. *Reports of the 1971 Advisory Council on Social Security.* (92nd Cong., 1st sess. H. Doc. 92-80.) Washington: U.S. G. P. O., 1971.

## II. Current Issues in Policy

Burns, Eveline M. *Social Security and Public Policy.* New York: McGraw-Hill Book Company, Inc., 1956.
Although written fifteen years ago, this thorough study by a leading scholar in the field of social security covers the essential and continuing issues in the field.

Haber, William, and Wilbur J. Cohen, eds. *Social Security Programs, Problems and Policies: Selected Readings.* Homewood, Illinois. R. D. Irwin, 1960.
This comprehensive collection of readings brings together a wide spectrum of articles and documents of interest to the student of social security. The editors have been closely involved in the field since the earliest beginnings. William Haber was a member of the Advisory Council of 1937-38. Wilbur Cohen was on the staff of the Committee on Economic Security and has been intensively engaged in the planning and administration of the social security program ever since, culminating in distinguished service as U.S. Secretary of Health, Education and Welfare.

Bowen, William G., Frederick H. Harbison, Richard A. Lester, and Herman M. Somers, eds. *The Princeton Symposium on the American System of Social Insurance: Its Philosophy, Impact, and Future Development.* Held in

June, 1967, in honor of J. Douglas Brown. New York: McGraw-Hill Book Company, Inc., 1968.

A collection of papers by leading economists at a conference of social security specialists with discussion from diverse points of view.

Pechman, Joseph A., Henry J. Aaron, and Michael K. Taussig. *Social Security: Perspectives for Reform*. Washington, D.C.: Brookings Institution, 1968.

The most thorough recent study of the social security program by economists outside the Social Security Administration. Contains valuable analytical material. The proposals for change are influenced by an emphasis upon an economic approach to social security problems. Excellent statistical data and bibliography.

Somers, Herman Miles, and Anne Ramsay Somers. *Medicare and the Hospitals: Issues and Prospects*. Washington, D.C.: The Brookings Institution, 1967.

A discerning analysis of the problems of providing hospital care through social insurance under present conditions. The authors are leading specialists in the economics of health services. Herman Somers served on the Advisory Council of 1963-64, which recommended the enactment of the Medicare program as well as on many other advisory bodies in the field of health.

Myers, Robert Julius. *Medicare*. Published for McCahan Foundation, Bryn Mawr, Pa., by R. D. Irwin, Homewood, Ill., 1970.

A comprehensive study of the history and issues in Medicare by the actuary closest to the developing social security program from 1934 to 1970. Myers participated in the planning of old age insurance in 1934-35 and, for many years, was chief actuary in the Social Security Administration.

239

Skidmore, Max J. *Medicare and the American Rhetoric of Reconciliation*. University, Alabama: University of Alabama Press, 1970.

An interesting and detailed discussion of the years of political controversy which preceded the enactment of Medicare.

# INDEX

accrued liability, 98f

actuarial discount, 118

actuarial policy, 184-87

adequacy, concept of, 135ff

advisory councils, initiation of, 45f; membership, 46ff; policies and procedures, 49-54; staff support, 48f

Altmeyer, A. J., 15, 45

American Medical Association, 194f, 197

Armstrong, B. N., 8ff, 15ff, 22

assessment insurance, Medicare, 204f

automatic adjustments, 187

automatic adjustment of ceilings, 70ff

average-wage concept, 166ff

Ball, R. M., 44

bend points, 61, 168

benefit statistics, 168

boundary between assistance and insurance, 56ff

board of trustees, 192ff

Bruère, H., 47

Bugniazet, G. M., 46

Byrd, H. F., 46

Cardozo, B. N., 13, 22f

ceiling on coverage, 19, 68ff, 171f

ceiling on employers' contribution, 92f

child's benefit, 104f

Clark Amendment, 65ff

collection of contributions, 19f

company pension plans, coordination with OASDI, 68f; effectiveness of, 72ff; function of, 67f; public interest in, 72ff

compensation of doctors, 204, 225f

constitutionality, 10ff

contingency reserve, concept of, 182ff

contributions as taxes, 85-89

control of use, Medicare, 205-207

coordination in planning, 43f

Corwin, E. S., 12

cost-averaging, Medicare, 201f

cost-of-living adjustments, 168-71, 177f

cost-sharing ratio, 92

coverage of dependents, Medicare, 220f

coverage of disabled, Medicare, 219f

cumulative wage credits, 165

current redistribution, concept of, 181f

custodial care, 221f

death benefit, 32f; 1935 Act, 131f

deductibles, Medicare, 211ff, 215f

dependent parents, 141f

differential benefits, concept of, 163f

disability, duration of, 160f

"disability freeze," 156f

241